Entrepreneur
MAGAZINE'S

ULTIMATE

CREDIT and COLLECTIONS HANDBOOK

MICHELLE DUNN

EP Entrepreneur Press

Editorial Director: Jere Calmes
Cover Design: Beth Hansen-Winter
Composition: CWL Publishing Enterprises, Inc., Madison, Wisconsin, www.cwlpub.com

This publication is designed to provide accurate and authoritative information in regard to the subject matter covered. It is sold with the understanding that the publisher is not engaged in rendering legal, accounting, or other professional services. If legal advice or other expert assistance is required, the services of a competent professional person should be sought.

> –From a Declaration of Principles jointly adopted by a
> Committee of the American Bar Association and
> a Committee of Publishers and Associations

ISBN 1-59918-025-1

Library of Congress Cataloging-in-Publication Data

Dunn, Michelle A.
   Ultimate book of credit and collections / by Michelle Dunn.
     p. cm.
   ISBN 1-59918-025-1 (alk. paper)
   1. Credit--Management–Handbooks, manuals, etc. 2. Commercial credit–Handbooks, manuals, etc.
   3. Small business–Finance–Handbooks, manuals, etc.. 4. Collecting of accounts--Handbooks,
   manuals, etc. I. Title.
   HG3751.D86 2006
   658.8'8--dc22

(3101915434151 8)

                                        2006010474

10 09 08 07 06   10 9 8 7 6 5 4 3 2 1

Contents

How to Use This Book

I F YOU PICKED UP THIS BOOK, YOU HAVE A goal in mind. You want to have a successful business without having to worry about slow or nonpaying customers, or you already have a business and you have customers who owe you money.

In order for any policy or plan to work, you need to have a goal in mind. We will call this book our Success Plan. In order for your credit policy to work, you need to have a goal, and a plan to achieve your goal. Let's start with your main goal and break it down from there. Get out a piece of paper and write down your main goal—use my example here to create your success plan.

Your main goal may be: To create a credit policy that makes you more money and more sales.

The steps you have to take to make that goal a reality could be:

1. Create new customer forms that out-
line your payment terms and check credit references and credit history before extending credit.
2. Learn what your rights are as a business owner and what laws you must follow to enforce them.
3. Educate yourself, your staff, and your clients on how you want to be paid.
4. Hire a credit manager.

Now for each of these steps, you will take smaller steps to make them happen.

1. Create new customer forms that outline your payment terms and check credit history before extending credit.
   - Use the forms in this book and create "New Account Packets" for new customers.
   - Research your accounting and billing procedures and create terms that benefit you, your business, and your customers.
   - Check the "New Account Forms"

and the credit references for all new customers.

2. Learn what your rights are as a business owner and what laws you must follow to enforce them.
   - Use this book as a guide to see what laws apply to you and your business.
   - Check with my accountant and/or attorney in regard to your policies and make sure you are familiar with any special laws in your state or the states in which you do business.
3. Educate yourself, your staff, and your clients on how you want to be paid.
   - Make sure the payment terms you set for your business benefit you, your business, and your customers.
   - Make sure everyone in your employ is aware of what your terms are.
   - Make sure everyone in your employ knows what types of payment you accept.
   - Hang up a sign in your office or store outlining your terms.
4. Hire a credit manager.
   - Learn what a credit manager does.
   - Use the sample job description in this book to educate yourself on what is expected of a credit manager.
   - Have a credit policy in place before hiring your credit manager *or*, if they are experienced, have them help you set it up.

This is an easy breakdown of what you have to do to reach your main goal, which is: To create a credit policy that makes you more money and more sales.

If you are just starting your business and writing your business plan, you can incorporate much of this into your business plan to show the bank how you plan to make money to pay them back. If you have your plan broken down into details like this, it shows you have put some thought into your finances, and are serious about having a successful business.

If you have an existing business, write out this plan, and follow these steps—you will be able to reach your main goal much more easily than someone without a plan. You also may want to set a due date by which each item must be completed. This way you can measure your success, and see your results. Setting realistic due dates will help you to achieve your goals in a timely manner.

ACKNOWLEDGMENTS

There are always so many people to thank when you write a book; no book is the work of just one person.

I first and foremost want to thank Kevin Maass, Jonathan Linden, and Nathan Linden—without them, none of this would have been possible. Support is a wonderful thing.

I would like to thank Roger C. Parker who "introduced" me to Jere Calmes, at Entrepreneur Press. Jere is a dream to work with and I feel like I have a new friend. I want to thank Ron Young, also from Entrepreneur Press, for his legal expertise and help. Thank you to Karen Thomas who helped me with my manuscript and all the questions I had, and who is such an enthusiastic partner that she helped keep me motivated and excited! I want to thank Lourdes Lopez, my agent for this book, who worked with Entrepreneur

Press on all the contracts and legal issues so that I didn't have to.

Many thanks to the members of my Credit and Collections group, my friends who know just when I need to chat or leave the house of writing, to see some real living, breathing people. Special thanks to Marcia Rosen, Carole Abel, Stephanie Chandler, Amy Marchant, Pete Masterson, Kitty Werner, John Culleton, Norma Burns, Carolyn Howard-Johnson, Dan Poynter, Cheryl Microutsicos, Deb Berry, Brett Rabideau, Michael Solomon, Tim Paulsen, Christopher Knight, Karen Terry, Arlene Stoppe, Lynn Stevens, Gage, and Spaz. I thank everyone whom I e-mail and network with every day—we can all be successful if we work together!

How Debt and Credit Affect Small Business Owners

CHAPTER 1

What Is Debt?

WE ALL KNOW WHAT DEBT IS, BUT how does it affect an entrepreneur or small business owner? Debt can mean many things; the most common is that it is an obligation or promise to do something. It also can be money, goods, or services owed by one person or business to another.

Most of us are really only familiar with personal debt, not business debt. When you start your own business you need to be in control of your debt and not let it control your business. An easy way to do this is to gain control of your personal debt; this will help you understand how it works, and how it can be controlled on a larger scale. One way to evaluate your debt is to pull your credit report. Get a copy from all three credit agencies because the information contained on each report may be different. Something else you can do is to gather all your monthly bills and calculate your monthly expenses. Be sure to include food, entertainment, clothing, car expenses, and anything else your business or you personally pay for.

You will then see your total income and expenses. You want your total income to be more than your expenses. If you are not paying your bills on time and in full each month with the income you have, you need to decrease your expenses or increase your income. For example, when I sold my business and the buyer stopped making his monthly payment to me, I had to adjust my income until the situation could be resolved. Some of the things I did were:

- Cancelled cable TV
- Cancelled cell phone services
- Purchased clothes on eBay and in second-hand shops
- Downgraded my home phone to a basic service, cancelled caller ID and call waiting

Expenses		Income	
Rent	$	Income from a spouse	$
Electric	$	Income from your job	$
Cable TV	$	**Total**	$
Internet	$		
Home phone	$		
Cell phone	$		
Heat	$		
Groceries	$		
Entertainment	$		
Gas, oil, car expenses	$		
Plowing	$		
Trash removal	$		
Taxes	$		
Maintenance	$		
Clothing	$		
Kids, lunch, haircuts, day care	$		
Total	$		

Figuring out expenses and income

- Signed up for an online movie service rather than renting movies; this way it is a fixed monthly payment
- Had pot luck networking events at my home for a "cheap night out" and networking event
- Car pooled

WHAT ENTREPRENEURS NEED TO KNOW ABOUT DEBT

If you are just starting your business, you are about to begin accumulating your business debt. Your first debt might be your business loan. You also may require loans for equipment or training, which you will have to repay. This is your business debt.

The best thing you can do with debt is to keep on top of it. If you owe money, always make paying it back your first priority. When you apply for your business loan, have a plan already in place on how you will make the money to repay that loan. This will help you get approved for the loan and also guide you when it is time to pay it back. You will want to make sure your income is enough to pay back your debt. There are steps you can take to ensure this.

Good billing procedures and credit policy will help you to make more money quicker and have fewer bad debts. This will help your business maintain an even cash flow and be more successful.

You may want to develop a budget for your business. To do this look at how much money comes in and how much goes out, or how much you spend. List your income and then list your fixed expenses, costs that are the same each month, such as rent, mortgage, or insurance. Then list other expenses that might change each month, such as postage, advertising, or supplies. These are called variable expenses. This will help you analyze your income and prioritize it. A sample budget might look like this:

Income	$
Spending	$
Fixed expenses	$
Variable expenses	$
Total	$

Some things you can do to maintain an even cash flow are:

- Implement a credit policy
- Develop a budget
- Implement billing procedures
- Provide good quality work and follow through

GETTING OUT OF DEBT

If your business is already in debt, how can you get out of it? If you have already become indebted and cannot seem to pay your bills on time there are steps you can take to get out of debt and continue to make more money. Normally, if you find you are in debt, it is a result of spending more than you are bringing in. You now need to reverse that process. One way you can do that is to look at who owes you money.

The first thing you will want to do is look at your accounts receivables listing. How many of your customers owe you money? Why do they owe you money? Why are they past due? How late are their payments? If you take charge of your accounts receivables report and do some collection work on the money that is owed to you, you can have more money right away. You also will want to review each account that is past due. Don't continue to ship products or provide services to someone who owes you money. This is where having a sound credit policy comes into play. If you don't have a credit policy in place, you need to create or implement one immediately. You can do this by using my book, *Become the Squeaky Wheel, a Credit & Collections Guide for Everyone.* There are instructions on how to create and implement a credit policy that works for a large or small business.

The second thing you want to do is look at what your policies are for and your customers' terms and/or credit limits. What are your terms? If, for example, your terms are net 30 and you are not getting paid for 60 days, maybe you want to include a prepayment discount. This could be as small as 1 percent on balances paid before 30 days. This gives the customer an incentive to pay you early. If you change your payment terms, send out a notice to your customers and also change it on all your paperwork, such as your invoices, statements, and credit applications. This notice also could be in the form of an announcement or flyer and include a payment envelope. This will alert your customers about the change and prompt them to pay immediately.

Another way to try to get customers to pay on time is to implement a late fee. For example, any balance paid after 30 days will incur a 3 percent late fee. This will encourage customers to pay before the 30 days. They will see they can save money while getting you paid early or on time.

Remember to notify your customers of any changes in your terms. A cheap way to do this is through e-mail.

The third step you can take is to review your fees. You want to be making sure you are not losing money on any services or products you provide. Find out what your cost and profit is for each service or product you offer. Maybe you can lower some prices and maybe you need to raise some prices. Maybe you can offer a special deal combining two services or products for a discounted price to encourage some immediate cash flow to put toward your debt. You also should look at what you are spending your money on. Try to cut back as quickly as you can. The more you cut back, the sooner you will be out of debt. Stick with your reduced expenses and plan until your debt is well under control. Some examples of ways you can cut back on your debt are:

- Skip that expensive specialty coffee and order regular coffee or buy a travel mug and bring your own from home.
- Cut back on your phone bill by re-evaluating the package or bells and whistles you pay for, such as call waiting and caller ID. Only pay for what you and your business really need.
- Cut back on your cell phone use—do you use all the extra options you pay for? Is there a cheaper option that might work for you?
- Shop smart for your home and business supplies and compare prices.

STAYING OUT OF DEBT

Once you have gotten your business out of debt, excluding, say, your business loan or mortgage,

you want to stay out of debt. There are not many businesses out there that don't have any debt. You may always have a mortgage on your building or office, but as long as you are able to make those payments easily and without incurring much additional debt, you will be doing well.

To stay out of debt you need to make sure that the money coming in is more than enough to cover all the debt you have including paying yourself or employees. If it is not, then that is what you have to work on to keep your business out of debt.

Some ways to increase your cash flow include:

- Implement early payment discounts
- Charge late fees
- Keep on top of your accounts receivables and contact anyone who is even "a little" past due
- Have a credit policy in place
- Get a signed credit application
- Check references on all new accounts
- Get a signed contract or agreement outlining payment terms
- Set credit limits

When you do any of these things you have to stick to it! So many business owners implement some or all of the above policies and then don't stick to them, most times because they are so eager to make the sale. If you make the sale and then don't get paid, you didn't make any money. If you know you have a quality service or product, be confident that people will want to do business with you because of that, and will respect you more for having to fill out any paperwork in order to open an account. They will know you are serious about your business and dedicated to customer service. "You get what you pay for" is a common phrase in business; this is so true in terms of having a sound credit policy as well. A potential customer will know you are reputable, serious, and there for the long run if they have to fill out any paperwork to get credit with your company. Your chances of getting paid back on time and in full are much better than someone who just extends credit without gathering any information on the potential customer.

If you are serious about staying out of debt, you need to change your financial habits. One thing I did that works great is to stop using credit cards—use a debit card instead. This way you are only spending money that you have and not money you are borrowing at a high interest rate. The average rate charged by a credit card company is 18 percent. If you become past due on your payments that figure can be raised up to 28 percent! In order to avoid this or get out of this situation, pay off your credit cards; pay the minimum on all cards except the one with the highest interest rate. Pay more than the minimum on the card with the highest interest rate. Once that one is paid in full, move on to paying off the next highest interest rate, and continue to pay the minimum on your other cards. Do this until all your cards are paid in full, ending with the card that has the lowest interest rate. During this time, do not use the cards! Put them in the freezer or cut them up. You will save more money by paying off the highest-interest cards first. Try not to keep looking and obsessing about your balances. Just keep making regular payments and use your debit card for any future purchases and your balances will go down.

DEALING WITH CREDITORS

If you already own a business and are in debt and are not able to make some payments, you will have to deal with your creditors. This is always a scary proposition for any business owner. Owing money and having someone trying to collect from your business gives you the feeling of failure. Working night and day and still not being able to pay your bills is not the image you want to project. So, what can you do?

First, find all your debt, and put it in front of you. Organize it into piles based on interest rates and total amounts due. You will want to pay any debt that is charging you a high interest rate first. Your next step is to call each of the companies you owe money to and explain your situation and tell them you are working on getting this all paid and need their help. Tell them you are trying to work out a payment plan that reduces your debt to a manageable level. Some of them may offer to lower or drop the interest rate on the existing balance until you can get caught up, if you make regular payments. If you keep in contact with the creditors and let them know what is going on, you will have a much easier time than the business owner who does not contact them and just tries to pay sporadically as they can. Creditors truly appreciate this and will work with you if you contact them. Remember that a successful repayment plan requires regular, on time payments. Having a plan in place will eliminate stress but does not mean you can forget about it. A demonstrated pattern of timely payments can help you get credit in the future.

The next thing you want to do is make sure you are not incurring any additional debt while you work on the existing debt. Try to make all future orders COD or prepaid, or use a debit card that debits the money from your checking or savings account. Do not use credit cards. If you need to make changes in your business to save money, look around and see what you can cut back on. Do you buy your employees lunch every day? Try just buying them lunch on Fridays.

Another way to increase your cash flow is through your existing customers. Make sure all accounts are current and up to date. If they are not, you need to buckle down and get them that way. This is existing money on your books that you just need to collect so you can pay off your debts. You also could have your sales department have a contest—offer a lunch or gift certificate to a local restaurant to the salesperson who gets the most paid orders in 30 days. You can customize this to fit your business. Be enthusiastic and motivate your team. You also could run a special deal on your biggest profit item to generate a large flow of cash to put toward your debt. The best thing to do is include your employees, and let them know what is happening so you can work together. The more help you have, the quicker you will be out of debt. Set realistic goals for your employees to reach. Offer an incentive to motivate your employees to help you. Also, remember to check your bills—if you pay a credit card bill late they may raise your interest rate up to 21 to 28 percent! Make sure you are not being charged any "annual fees" or for any kind of "protection program" that you don't want.

HOW SMALL BUSINESS OWNERS CAN HANDLE BAD CREDIT

Having good credit is more important for a small business owner than a large one, though it is important for every business. But smaller businesses need credit to order supplies and sometimes to keep their business running. This is why good credit for your business is essential. The first thing you want to do is get a copy of your business's credit report; in some cases this will be your personal credit report. It is important to understand that if you own a business, its credit and payment history could be linked directly with your personal credit record, so you need to keep both clean. You can now get a copy of your reports from all three credit bureaus for free once a year.

Equifax
P.O. Box 740241
Atlanta, GA 30374-0241
(800) 685-1111

Experian
P.O. Box 2002
Allen, TX 75013
(888) 397-3742

TransUnion
P.O. Box 1000
Chester, PA 19022
(800) 916-8800

There is also a link to a central site that allows you to request a free credit file disclosure, commonly called a credit report, once every 12 months from each of the nationwide consumer credit reporting companies: Equifax, Experian, and TransUnion. Visit their web sites for more information. You also can request your report by phone or mail. Monitoring and periodically reviewing your credit report is also an effective tool in fighting identity theft. Look for old or inaccurate information and contest it if it is not correct. Send the credit agency a letter in writing and include your complete name, address, and each item you are disputing. Send a copy of your credit report with the disputed item circled or highlighted. Be sure to make a copy for yourself before you mail the information and send the letter by certified mail.

Once you receive your reports, look them over and find where your bad credit is. Contact those companies and get copies of what is past due. Work with them to get those debts paid and reported as such on your credit report. If some of the debts are old or mostly interest with little principal, some companies will accept a settlement amount. If you decide to pay a settlement amount, it will be reported on your credit report as a "settlement." You also can include a letter to be attached to your credit report if you dispute any of the debts that are listed there. Contact the credit bureau that has the debt listed and they will give you the address you need to send a letter explaining why the debt is disputed. Once you do this, when someone pulls your report to check your credit, they are supposed to ignore that item and not let it influence their credit-making decision. On the next page you will find a sample letter you can use.

It is very important that you keep a copy of your letter and continue to follow up with the agency until what you requested has been done. The credit reporting agency must investigate your claim, normally within 30 days. They will contact the provider that gave them the information and request it to be verified. Anything you dispute that the credit bureau cannot verify must be deleted from your report. Once the credit agency investigates your claim they must give you written results. You also can request that the credit bureau notify anyone who received a copy of your credit report in the last six months of the change. If you have been denied credit and are disputing an item, you may want to send a copy of the dispute letter to any creditors who denied you credit based on the disputed item.

PROTECT YOURSELF AND YOUR BUSINESS FROM IDENTITY THEFT

Identity theft is America's fastest growing type of robbery. There have been an estimated 9.9 million victims in America and over 40 percent of all consumer complaints in the United States involve identity theft. About half of the victims do not know how the thief obtained their personal information. The *Boston Globe* and *Newsweek* have both covered identity theft issues in 2005 telling us how important it is to educate ourselves on preventing and protecting ourselves from this type of robbery. Identity theft can happen anytime, anywhere, and to anyone, individuals or businesses. Everyone must be educated and aware so it can be avoided. A U.S. Postal Inspector has said that postal money orders and business or certified checks are one way you can be at risk. Most identity theft involves the U.S. Mail, which is why the U.S. Postal Inspection Service is a lead agency in investigating identity theft. Identity theft is a criminal offense.

Some scams are Internet related—you go into a chat room and chat with people there, someone approaches you as a friend, or about an auction. You become comfortable with the people you are chatting with and start a "friendship." The person who has befriended you may tell you such things as, "I am in the Peace Corp, and I have a money order that I can't cash where I am," which is Lagos or Nigeria. They might ask you, if they send you the money order, if you will cash it and send them the money. This is a scam. The money order you receive can be fraudulent. Once you cash the money order and send the money you are out this money once the bank realizes the order was no good.

Another scenario might be if you sell items at online auctions. Someone may e-mail you about your item that is for sale. They will tell you they want to purchase your item, and they are in Nigeria so they will send you extra money to pay for a shipper to send the item to them. They will send you a counterfeit money order or check and ask you to cash the check and wire the extra money to them so they can pay the shippers to ship your item. They may even ask you to go to a bank to cash the money order rather than the post office. The reason for this is that the post office has a machine that can tell if the money order is counterfeit, and they have much more experience with money orders than banks.

Many of these types of scams originate in Nigeria, London, and Toronto. If you are aware of this, you can prevent it from happening to you. Most thieves still obtain personal information through traditional rather than electronic channels. In the cases where the method was known, 68.2 percent of information was obtained offline versus only 11.6 percent obtained online.

If you receive a fraudulent money order and take it to a bank, rather than the post office, a bank can take a month or more before they notify you that the money order is counterfeit. If this happens, you are then responsible for the funds. If you do get caught up in this situation, take your money order to a post office rather than a bank—it does not guarantee you will not be "taken" but it lowers your chances.

How to Tell if a Money Order Is Fraudulent

Fake money orders do not have a water mark. Hold up the money order to the window or light and look for a portrait on the left side. This portrait needs to be backlit to be seen and cannot be mimicked. Some producers of fraudulent money orders try to use fake pictures as a water mark; you will be able to tell the difference if you hold it to the light. These money orders are generally printed in Nigeria. They use the same offset press we use to print real money orders, so check your money orders! You also can check for type size, color, and fonts. Another step you can take is to call or go online to the post office and give them the serial number of the money order; they can tell if it is real. If you receive a counterfeit money order, you will want to give it to the post office or police. Possession of a counterfeit item is a felony. If you give the money order to the post office or police, keep a copy for your records.

Other scams include receiving an e-mail or letter stating you have won a lottery, or a prize notification. Some letters or announcements will arrive with a counterfeit check and you pay a processing fee to get the prize. These checks are counterfeit; never send money to anyone who is asking for money from you in order to give you money, whether it is disguised as a prize or a lottery. Any prize that requires you to pay anything is no prize.

How These People Get Your Name

If you have a credit card, your name is sold to third parties. If you do not want this to happen, you must contact your credit card companies to inform them that you do not want your information sold. Check the privacy notice that comes with your bill—you know, all the extra slips of paper you receive with your credit card bill. Normally you throw those away, but check them for your privacy notice. If you enter contests, your information becomes public. Also, when you buy a new product, and fill out the warranty cards, those companies sell that information you provide to other companies. Since when does your toaster manufacturer need to know your household's annual income to extend a warranty on your toaster? Thieves use dumpster digging, *phishing*, and *pharming* to obtain your information. Things identity thieves steal from your trash include:

- **Pre-approved credit card offers**—they complete them and have the card sent to them at a different address.
- **Loan applications**—they complete the application and have the money sent to a phony address.
- **Bank statements**—they then have your bank account number and can print counterfeit checks.

One consumer credit counselor knew of someone who had their wallet stolen, and the thieves used the credit card to buy a $5,000 gift card at Wal-Mart—this then became very hard to trace.

People who are more at risk are senior citizens, people with disabilities, and immigrants—but remember that everyone, including children, is at risk. Senior citizens are home all day; they might get a phone call from a fake charity asking for money. Immigrants are desperate for credit; they may have just arrived in the United States and know they need credit to do anything and are not aware of these scams. People with disabilities are home and may become victims of phone or online fraud. There also have been cases of home-care providers taking advantage of their clients. Remember, it is not always a stranger who can steal someone's identity. Did you know children can be victims of identity theft? This could affect or ruin their credit before they even are able to build up credit for themselves. There have been cases of parents using a child's name for their electric bill or phone bill when they have bad credit or owe the utility company money. Thieves will obtain the Social Security number of these children and use that number to get credit cards and rack up purchases.

Some of these scammers will call you and say they are from a fictitious charity. They will offer to have your contribution automatically deducted from your checking account and will ask for your routing number, bank name, and account number. **Do Not Give Out This Information!** If you pick up a call from a telemarketer, ask them the following questions and if they are a fraud, they will hang up quickly.

- Who do you work for? (They will try to give you the name of the fake charity here, so ask them who pays their salary.)

- How much of my donation (percentage) goes to this charity and what is the rest of the money used for? If they are for real, they can easily give you this information.
- What is the charity's full name, address, and phone number?

Once you have the above information you can check with the state Attorney General's office or Secretary of State to see if the charity is registered. Also check the charity's rating through the Better Business Bureau at www.give.org.

How to Prevent Identity Theft from Happening to You and Your Business

Never leave your receipt or slip in the ATM or gas pump. Pay attention to your habits, and lock up or organize and file your bills and bank statements. Shred them using a cross-shredder before throwing them away.

In a recent article in *MSN Money*, research showed that 32 percent of people said they had been a victim of identity fraud by a friend or family member, and 13 percent were victimized by a co-worker. Beware! These people know your patterns and habits.

Some steps you can take to avoid becoming a victim of identity theft are:

- Get a copy of your credit report from all three credit bureaus. (FREE as of 9/1/05)
  - Experien, P.O. Box 2002, Allen, TX 75013, www.experian.com (888) 397-3742
  - Equifax, P.O. Box 740241, Atlanta, GA 30348, www.equifax.com (800) 685-1111

- TransUnion, P.O. Box 4000, Chester, PA 19016, www.transunion.com (866) 887-2673
- Opt out of mailing lists by contacting the credit bureaus above.
- Opt out by reading the privacy notice that comes with your credit card and following the instructions.
- Call the national Do Not Call Registry at (888) 382-1222 or visit www.donotcall.gov. Be sure to call from the number you want to register.
- Do not carry your Social Security Card in your wallet.
- Do not print your Social Security number on your checks.
- Do not get your Social Security number printed on your driver's license.
- Do not carry your Medicaid card with you as Medicaid policy numbers are your Social Security number.
- Delete any e-mails or lottery or prize notifications from Nigeria. Do not open.
- Stop credit card offers by contacting (888) 5-OPT-OUT.
- Remove your name from national mailing lists by visiting www.the-dma.org or write to Mail Preference Service, P.O. Box 643, Carmel, NY 10512.
- Install firewall and virus protection software on your computer.
- Password protect your computer and private personal files.
- Format your hard drive or physically destroy it when disposing of your old computer.

- When you order new checks, get your first initial printed on them instead of your first name.
- Use a cross-shredder to shred your bills and bank statements or any junk mail.
- Bring your mail to the post office or secure mail box rather than leaving it in a rural box.
- Use only one designated credit card for online purchases.
- Be sure all online purchases are made through a secure server—notice the "lock" icon and how the URL address changes from http to https. The *s* means *secure*.
- Do not carry your personal identification number (PIN) in your wallet.
- Do not use your date of birth as a password or PIN.
- Do not give out personal or financial information over the phone.
- Grind up or shred backup CDs or tapes you are throwing away.
- Check your online banking account at least three times a week and change your password often.

There is a new bill that is being passed. It is a very weak bill but if passed, it will prohibit using a Social Security number for identification purposes. This bill took effect in 2006.

If you feel you have been a victim of identity fraud, contact the Department of Justice, Consumer Protection division. They offer mediation with identity theft; they also have a hot line for consumers available 8 A.M. to 5 P.M. Monday through Friday. They maintain a database of written complaints dating back to 1998. They also offer seminars to schools, seniors, or any legitimate group.

Be aware that 40 million crooks obtained credit card numbers this past year. *Be suspicious.* Also be aware that most identify theft is not reported, especially when it involves family members, so the statistics are not completely accurate. These statistics show that consumers lost $5 billion last year when in actuality it is closer to $50 billion. There have been an estimated 9.9 million victims in America.

What to Do if You or Your Business Is a Victim of Identity Theft

- Contact the fraud departments of the three major credit bureaus, to place a fraud alert on your credit file.
- Close all accounts that have been affected and request copies of fraud-dispute forms and complete and return immediately. Keep copies!
- File a police report in each jurisdiction the theft occurred.
- Send copies of the report to your creditors or anyone who requires proof of the crime.
- File a complaint with the FTC (800-IDTHEFT or www.consumer.gov/idtheft) and the local post office.
- Contact the Identity Theft Resource Center at (858) 693-7935 or www.idtheftcenter.org.
- Request a new driver's license from the state motor vehicles department and have a fraud report attached to your driving record.
- Notify check-verification firms about any fraudulent checks:

- International Check Service (800) 526-5380
- Telecheck (800) 927-0755
- Certegy Check Services (800) 437-5120
- Call (888) CALL-FCC and file a complaint.

Change your password(s) and PIN immediately.

What Is *Phishing*?

If you get an e-mail, letter, or form that looks like it came from your bank, credit card company, the IRS, online auction, or bill paying service asking you to verify information so they can update their records, verify this with your bank or credit card company. Never click on the link in an e-mail; it will take you to a fraudulent web site that is disguised to look like the specific company's site. If you call to verify and your bank or credit card company wants this information, give it to them over the phone if you initiated the call and are sure it is the correct number, or stop by in person if possible.

There are warning signs to look for to identify scams. If someone tells you: "Poor or no credit?—No problem!," "Credit problems? No problem!," "We can erase bad credit, guaranteed!," "Create a new credit identity, legally!," "We can remove bankruptcies, judgments, liens, and bad loans from your credit report forever!," do not proceed. If someone offers you a "bargain loan," rushes you through the application process, or wants you to pay a fee, do not do business with them. If a salesperson comes to your door and says, "I was just in the neighborhood…," do not believe them. Only time, effort, and a well thought out plan will improve your credit report. Remember, if it sounds too good to be true, it is!

AVOIDING SCAMS

If you decide to hire a company to help you get out of debt, be careful. Before you do business with any company check their references, contact the Better Business Bureau where they are located and see if they are a member of any organizations, such as a trade association or chamber of commerce. Some examples of terminology used by some "credit repair" companies might be:

- "Consolidate your bills into 1 monthly payment."
- "STOP collection agency harassment."
- "Wipe out your debt—consolidate your bills."

Some companies use those headlines to grab your attention and then try to get you to file for bankruptcy, which can hurt your credit and cost you attorney's fees. If you find a company you feel is legitimate, make sure they don't:

- Want you to pay for credit repair services up front
- Omit telling you your legal rights and what you can do for free
- Recommend that you don't contact your creditors or the credit bureaus

Credit repair companies cannot:

- Make false claims about their services
- Charge you before completing their services
- Provide any services without a signed, written contract

If you do sign a contract with a credit repair company, make sure that the contract:

- Specifies the total cost and breakdown of costs involved

- Includes a very detailed description of the services they will provide
- States how long the process will take. Try to include an actual completion date.
- Includes their full business name, business mailing and physical address, e-mail address, and phone numbers

If you have been a victim of a scam contact your state's Attorney Generals office or the Better Business Bureau immediately.

CHAPTER 2

What Is Credit?

WHEN YOU MENTION THE WORD credit the first thing that comes to most people's minds is "bad." Credit means so many things but in this book we are talking about your business credit. This can mean money available for a customer to borrow in some cases. If you extend credit, you are letting someone borrow money from you with the promise of a payback. You are deferring payment with strict terms of repayment. Extending credit is a privilege you granted for the purpose of extending time to make payment on a debt.

A good way to understand what extending credit is about is to look at it this way. Someone comes into your store or office, and they decide on a product or service, say a television or to have some copies made. You talk to them, they pick something out, they load the TV into their truck or pick up the 500 copies and they say, "I'll be back tomorrow to pay for this."

If you don't have a credit policy or check credit, that is what you are doing, just giving your work away to strangers for free. You don't know this person, so at the very least get a credit application filled out. In my years in the collection industry, I have seen so many situations like the one just described. Companies would place accounts with me to collect on and sometimes not even have a last name. Don't let this happen to you, you deserve to be paid. You put a lot of work and thought into starting and running your business, don't let credit be the cause of a failure.

▼ MAKE MONEY, NOT FRIENDS

Remember, you are in business to make money, not friends. A lot of friends will be made through doing business, but that is not why you are in business.

HOW CREDIT AFFECTS SMALL BUSINESSES

If you don't have a credit policy, everyone will want to buy from you. This can result in unpaid and past due invoices on your books. Business owners sometimes make common mistakes when they are starting out. Most new businesses depend on their income more than anyone else, because it is so sporadic. There is no set weekly paycheck, at least not in the beginning. Many new business owners are so eager to make a sale;, they will extend credit on a promise of payment without getting any information from the customer. They are afraid to appear too needy or they may think asking for any additional information might offend the potential customer and they will go somewhere else. This is not the case. Any customer who balks at having to fill out any paperwork to receive a credit account is not worth having as a customer.

▼ **TOP FOUR COLLECTION MISTAKES**

1. No credit policy in place

2. Extending credit to anyone who walks in the door

3. Not using a credit policy to make more money and sales

4. Receiving too many NSF notices or bad checks

You *always* want to have a written contract, agreement, or at the very least a signed credit application. If the sale is for a large amount of money, maybe you want to get half or a large portion of the money up front. You can set special terms and have specific contracts or agreements for large purchases. When financing a larger purchase some common terms are half down at the time of the order and the balance at the time of completion unless you want to break the final payment into two, three, or even four smaller payments. If you extend credit without getting a credit application filled out, customers know you aren't serious about your money or your business and this could lead to payment issues down the road.

This is not the only type of credit you and your business need to be concerned with. If you take the steps outlined in this book, you will be able to maintain a good credit history for your business, which will result in more success for you.

If you set up a credit policy and check your customers' information before extending any credit to them, you will be able to maintain your bills and therefore maintain a good credit report for your business. This is essential to keep your business going. You will need to apply for credit with suppliers and maybe a credit card company or a loan for your business. If your customers are not paying you in a timely manner, you will not be able to pay your creditors on time. Remember that no business is protected from bad debt, including yours. You can protect yourself and your business by taking these steps:

- Having a sound credit policy and sticking to it
- Getting a signed credit application
- Checking references

- Getting a signed contract or agreement
- Pulling a credit report if possible
- Setting realistic credit limits

HOW SMALL BUSINESS OWNERS CAN GET CREDIT

Starting your business is overwhelming in itself, never mind having to think about credit. Your business will need good credit to maintain itself and become more successful. You can get and maintain good credit for your business a few different ways. You might be applying for a small business loan to get your business started; this will show on your credit report. Make sure if you take out a loan to start your business, it is a payment you can realistically make and make on time every month. Try to pay it off early if you can. Realize this will be your most important payment each month and make it the first bill you pay each month. You also may apply for credit with suppliers; this can build up some credit so that you can apply for a business credit card down the line. If you purchase supplies for your business, such as restroom supplies, office supplies, or shop supplies, ask the suppliers if you can apply for a charge account, where you can order and receive a bill from which to pay. This will build up credit with them and down the line you can use them as a credit reference, provided you pay them on time. When you apply for a business credit card, you can list your business loan and these suppliers as references; even if you only get a small amount of credit extended to you, it can grow with time as your business grows.

If your suppliers offer you credit and send you an invoice, notice if they offer an early pay-ment discount. If the terms are net 30 but there is a 2 percent discount if you pay within 15 days, take advantage of that. It will reflect on your business credit report and save you money. Remember, if they had not extended you credit, you would have been paying the full amount up front to get your goods, so this is just another way your business can make more money. As your business grows, this amount becomes larger thus saving you more and more the bigger you get.

THE IMPACT OF BAD CREDIT ON YOUR SMALL BUSINESS

When you are just starting your business, you are better off not even applying for or getting credit if you don't think you can pay it back right away. No credit is better than bad credit. Once you have bad credit, from not paying your suppliers on time or at all, you incur late fees, and lose your credit and credibility. You then lose any discounts you might have been able to take advantage of and you lose a credit reference, affecting any future credit you might apply for. Though it is illegal to publish the names of people or businesses that don't pay, or are late payers, word gets around in any industry.

If you can't afford to buy on credit or don't have the references to apply for credit, just purchase your supplies from your creditors while pre-paying or COD for as long as you have to. Just doing this will create a credit history with that company. Then once you do apply, you might be able to get credit through that company on your merits with them alone. You can easily create credit for your small business, but it is much harder to correct bad credit once you have created it.

> ## ▼ PROVIDE WHAT IS NEEDED!
>
> The key to your success will be to find out what is needed and provide it.

WHY YOU SHOULD EXTEND CREDIT

Extending credit works in your favor in many ways.

- It increases customer loyalty.
- If you have credit applications for new customers to fill out, they know you plan to be around for a while and that you are interested in your customers. They feel like getting credit is a favor you do for them and they like that idea.
- It shows your business as financially stable; it tells your customers that you care and are serious about your money, success, clientele, and future.
- It increases your sales, and therefore your bottom line.
- Studies show customers will purchase more if they can pay later.
- It shows you are serious and smart about your business.
- You are not desperate, otherwise you would extend credit to anyone who walked in your door.
- It allows you to expand your customer base.
- Customers who are happy with your terms will tell other people about you. Word-of-mouth advertising is the best and cheapest advertising there is. Offer incentives or discounts for referrals of other credit-approved customers.
- It shows good customer service.
- It shows you are interested in your customer and want to help them by offering sales and discounts and a credit limit so they can buy more now and pay later.

WHY YOUR CUSTOMERS WANT YOU TO EXTEND CREDIT

- Convenience, they can write one check a month, rather than every time they order something from you.
- They may not have the money right now but will soon and need your service or product now. We live in a world of "I want it now." Credit allows us to fulfill this need.
- They feel it makes them an "official" customer. They go through a process to get credit from you, you know personal financial information about them, and you created an account for them in your computer. They also will feel that if they are not happy with something, such as customer service, delivery, or quality, they can withhold payment until the issue is resolved. They will feel like they are a valued customer whom you will listen to if they have an issue.
- It creates a paper trail.
- It makes them feel important; when you extend credit you extend faith in your customer.

When you extend credit, it will increase your customers' loyalty. When you approve someone for credit, they feel happy, like they won something. They feel connected to you and will buy from you before the competition because they feel as though you trust them enough to allow them extra time to pay and maybe you set a credit limit that allows them to purchase more from you at one time, since they have a little more time to pay. When you extend credit it also shows potential clients and customers that you are not a sinking ship. You can afford to sell them something and wait for your money, within your terms of course. Customers who are given 30 days or even 15 days to pay are very appreciative.

Extending credit and offering reasonable credit limits also increases your sales. Some customers may be unable to pay for a product or service in its entirety, especially if it is a larger purchase of, say, a piece of equipment that they might need to start their own business, or a heating system, or something large that isn't a normal everyday expense. If they have the option to pay for this in monthly or weekly installments, they will be more inclined to make larger purchases that do not fall within their current budget to pay all at once but for which they are able to swing payments. They also then may feel a certain loyalty to you and become a long-standing customer. Some customers look at it as you extending them a personal favor. When they were in a bind and needed this expensive product, you trusted them enough to let them pay on account. Quite a few customers will always remember that and spread the word. The key is to be smart about it and only extend credit to those who qualify. Remember, the bottom line is that you are in business to make money, not friends. A lot of friends are made through a business, but that is not why you are in business.

There are some downfalls to extending credit; you could lose interest that you might have earned by having them pay in full and putting that money in a savings account, even if it is low interest. You might not be able to take advantage of purchase discounts from your vendors if the funds are not immediately available to you. You may end up lacking capital to start your next job if your customers are paying on account. You need to look at your situation and each extension of credit to make sure it is reasonable and will be profitable for your business.

HOW AND WHEN TO EXTEND CREDIT

When you decide to extend credit to your customers, you will need to decide on how you want to extend that credit. You don't want to be too lenient or too strict. If you are too lenient you could create a credit loss or bad debt. If you are too strict, it could affect sales. You will want your terms to be acceptable to your customers. Try to do some research in the area of your expertise, or your business. See what other business owners in your field give for credit terms or if they extend credit at all. Any information you can find out will help you. For example, say you have an auto shop, and you find out there is another auto shop in your area that only accepts cash, no checks or credit cards and no credit. You will want to offer credit, payment with checks, and credit cards. If you make yourself different by offering something that is missing in your industry, you will obtain more customers and be more successful. The key is to find out what is needed and provide it.

Do a search online and look for your industry or your business. For example, when I was starting my collection agency, I typed in *collection agency and debt collection.* Hundreds of sites came up. Visit those sites and see how they are set up and laid out. See if you can request information from them through their web site. Some of the site owners will e-mail you the information and others will mail you information. Create a folder of all the pertinent correspondence you receive. Once you feel you have enough information, go through your folder and make a list of:

1. The common services they all offer
2. The different pricing structures
3. Any different offers, such as 24/7 customer service, or online chat support

From this list, determine what is *not* being offered by any of these companies, and try to incorporate that into your business. Highlight that special feature that only you offer on your web site, flyers, and business card. Be the only one or the first one to offer what is lacking from your competitors. If you do this, you will get more customers because you offer something different. Check out what customers get for the price they pay, do not set your price lower than everyone else, and try to be in the middle of the road if you can. If you feel you offer something exceptional, charge a higher price. Remember, you get what you pay for; cheaper is not always better.

You and your staff must stand behind your credit policy, even if your credit policy is just having every new customer fill out a credit application. Make no exceptions. Blame it on someone else if it makes you uncomfortable, but do it! Sales departments hate asking customers for credit applications, they spend their day trying to make the sale, only to find out the customer is denied the credit. Tell them they can blame you, or the

accountant, if it makes them uncomfortable. Extending credit to someone with a bad or non-existent credit history can be the equivalent of working for free.

All departments must support and abide by the credit rules you set or your credit policy will not work. If everyone doesn't support the policy this will result in your business credit suffering, your profits being affected, and your relationships with vendors suffering.

HOW TO MANAGE YOUR CUSTOMERS SO THEY DON'T MANAGE YOU

As I mentioned earlier, if you don't tell your customers how and when you want to be paid, they are left to decide how and when to pay you. If you don't tell them how long they have to pay, how can you penalize them for paying late? They won't know when "late" is. Some steps you can take to manage your customers and cash flow are:

1. Give your credit policy the priority it deserves.
2. Establish your credit policy as a matter of company policy.
3. Educate your staff, suppliers, vendors, and customers about your credit policy.
4. Always be professional.
5. Check customers' credit and/or references, including industry and bank references and/or pulling credit reports.
6. Establish credit limits and stick to them!
7. Review credit histories and limits once a year or more if you suspect your customer may have financial difficulties.
8. Keep in contact and be aware of activity on larger accounts.

9. Send invoices immediately when work is complete.

10. Charge late fees or penalties on past due accounts and enforce them.

11. Accept as many payment options as you can: credit and debit cards, checks, online payments.

12. Monitor your accounts receivables reports and take action on past due accounts immediately.

The longer someone owes you money, the less the chance you will get paid. When you don't treat past due balances as important enough to make an effort to collect, the customer assumes that it is not important. They figure if you don't say anything you either don't care, it's not that important to you, or you're not worried about it.

FIFTEEN REASONS WHY YOU NEED A CREDIT POLICY

1. You will use the letters and forms to collect on past due accounts.

2. You can use the sample credit applications to take control of your cash flow today.

3. You will learn how to handle and avoid NSF and other returned checks.

4. You will learn how to extend credit so that it makes you more money.

5. You will learn how to pull credit reports and how to read them.

6. You will learn how to communicate with your customers to help them stay current.

7. You will learn how to make more money by controlling your cash flow.

8. You can take advantage of discounts to make you more money.

9. You will learn how to effectively do business online.

10. You will be able to use small claims court to your advantage.

11. You can check out credit and collections resources online that will jump-start your cash flow.

12. You will learn how discounts and late fees can increase early and on-time payments.

13. You will learn how a collection agency can work for you.

14. You will know what to do if your customer dies or goes bankrupt.

15. You will learn how to set up payment arrangements that benefit your cash flow and make your business a success.

CHAPTER 3

Avoiding Pitfalls for Any Small Business

SMALL BUSINESS OWNERS SOMETIMES make common mistakes when just starting out, and trying to get paid. Some small business owners depend on that income more than someone who gets a check each week. This is because when you work for yourself, the work and therefore the payments are sporadic.

Small business owners just starting out are sometimes so eager to make a sale that they will accept work or an order without getting a signed contract or checking credit references. They just wait and wait to be paid because they don't want to offend the customer or appear that they *need* the money.

Always get a written contract or agreement; you also may want to get half of the money up front with terms regarding the balance very specifically addressed in your agreement. If you can get the other party to sign the agreement, that is even better. I never do any work or business with anyone, even a friend, without a contract.

It is worth it to try and collect the money due at first. Make a couple of calls, but if promises are made but no payment is received, think about using a collection service. It shows you are serious and don't work for free. Word will get around that you mean business.

How do you avoid bad debt? There are some steps you can take to avoid bad debt, which result in your making more money with your business. Your company is not protected from bad debt, so you need to protect yourself by:

- Having a sound credit policy and sticking to it
- Getting a signed credit application
- Checking references
- Getting a signed contract or agreement
- Pulling a credit report if possible
- Setting a credit limit

Be firm about being paid from the beginning. If a debtor knows you are serious, they will be more likely to pay. If they had to fill out a credit application and/or contract, it shows you're serious. If you place accounts for collection sooner than later, that also shows you mean business.

Debtors will know you are serious if:

- They have to fill out a credit application
- They have to sign a contract
- They receive invoices right away
- You send your invoices right away, as soon as items have shipped or the work is complete
- You call right away if you don't receive payment. Don't wait!
- You gather all the information you can about the debtor before making a sale
- You are professional at all times
- You are persistent
- You make personal visits when you can
- You offer different payment methods
- You charge a late fee and/or finance charge

Some ways to avoid credit pitfalls when you are starting your business are:

- Get a signed contract or agreement.
- Get half or most of the money up front for large purchases and only extend credit on smaller balances.
- Have every customer fill out and sign a credit application.
- Make sure to get multiple contact information for each customer, such as home and work address, home phone number, work number, cell number, and e-mail address.
- Check *all* references: bank, suppliers, and personal. Make notes and keep them in the customer's file.

- Mail your invoices or statements immediately and consistently.
- Follow up immediately if a payment is late or a partial payment is received.

Also remember to:

- Be persistent.
- Be professional at all times.
- Make personal visits, or be available. If your customers see you at the coffee shop or buying the paper, and you say hello, they are more apt to pay you since they see you more often than a vendor whom they don't even know or never see.
- Offer different payment options; some customers may end up with a cash-flow problem but might have a credit card they can make a payment with.
- Charge a late fee or finance charge.

You should remember that you cannot and will not collect on *every* account. Think of those customers as a cost of doing business. Learn from them and know that success feeds on your credit and collections policy.

Be involved with your customers and/or your community. If your customers see you and know who you are they will be less likely to avoid paying you or to pay you late. If they start paying late and you see them when you are buying coffee, you can ask them to stop by later to your office or shop. Sometimes just that will result in a payment being forthcoming and future payments being made on time. If your clients are not in your general area, and seeing them locally is not an option, be sure to call them or e-mail them. Send them cards when appropriate; say, when they make their twenty-fifth payment, or when they pay off the debt. You could say something like, "Congratulations! You are halfway there, and we appreciate your prompt payments and business." You can even offer them a coupon or promotional item, such as a notepad with your company name on it. This notepad will end up on their desk with your company name on it, they will read it all the time so they will think about your business often and be reminded that they owe you money. They will appreciate that you have noticed they are making timely payments and that you appreciate them as a customer, and this will help ensure all future payments are made on time.

If you e-mail or talk to your clients, make notes on their account when they mention something personal, such as their child being accepted to a school or graduating. Send a card showing that you listen to them when they talk to you and that you remembered. Many businesses don't do this so you will stand out and get paid before all others. Try to purchase items or services from your customers if you can. If you buy from them and pay on time they will move your bills to the top of the pile, since, if they are late, they not only lose a vendor or supplier but a customer as well.

OUTSOURCE OR IN-HOUSE?

Many business owners starting their own business are starting a business based on what they know and what they enjoy and are good at. This usually doesn't involve credit or debt collection. Credit and debt collection go along with every business just like taxes. It is a lot to learn and keep up on. Some businesses decide to maintain their credit policy and collections inhouse. Some business owners may do it themselves or hire someone to do it for them. Others will outsource it just like they outsource their taxes or the cleaning of their office. The choice is a personal one. If you are not so busy when you first start up your business, it is a good idea to do it yourself and it will make you familiar with how it all works and how you want it to work for you. This also helps when you do decide to outsource your credit and debt collection because you will know what you want the company to do for you. You will know what is expected and will be able to make a more educated decision on which company you will outsource to.

You can hire a credit manager to handle all aspects of your new clients: billing, collections, credit limits, credit reports, and disputes. If you do this, you have to make sure that whoever you hire is well versed in the laws surrounding this area. Some important things a credit manager must be familiar with to serve you in the best possible way are:

- Formal credit policies; see my book *Become the Squeaky Wheel, a Credit and Collections Guide for Everyone*
- Ability to generate cash flow with prompt payments being made
- Credit and collections training, see *www.credit-and-collections.com*
- Fair Debt Collection Practices Act
- Fair Credit Reporting Act
- Local and state laws
- Federal laws
- The Truth in Lending Act
- The Fair Credit Billing Act
- The Equal Credit Opportunity Act

The Fair Debt Collection Practices Act is geared mostly toward third-party collectors. Small business owners are more directly affected by state laws that apply directly to collection methods used by a creditor, though every credit manager needs to be extremely familiar with this Act. Some states mirror parts of this Act in laws within their states.

The Fair Credit Reporting Act regulates anyone who does any credit reporting to consumers' credit reports, good or bad. This Act is intended to protect consumers from having their eligibility for credit marred by incomplete or misleading credit report information. The laws give consumers the right to a copy of their credit reports. If they see inaccurate items, they can ask that the report be corrected or removed. If the business reporting the credit problem doesn't agree to a change or if the credit bureau refuses to make it, the consumer can add a 100-word statement to the file explaining their side of the story. This then becomes a part of any future credit report.

Local and state laws vary in each and every state. Some states are beginning to mirror federal laws. You will need to be familiar with the state laws where you are located and where your customers are located, if they are not in the same state. You can go to any state's web site for the attorney general's office and find this information or even call and have them mail you information. Some states' web sites are listed below.

Alabama	www.alabama.gov
Alaska	www.state.ak.us
Arizona	www.az.gov
California	www.ca.gov/state
Colorado	www.colorado.gov
Connecticut	www.ct.gov
Delaware	www.delaware.gov
Florida	www.myflorida.com
Georgia	www.georgia.gov
Hawaii	www.ehawaiigov.org
Idaho	www.accessidaho.org
Illinois	www.illinois.gov
Indiana	www.state.in.us
Iowa	www.state.ia.us
Kansas	www.accesskansas.org
Kentucky	www.ky.gov
Louisiana	www.state.la.us
Maine	www.state.me.us
Maryland	www.maryland.gov
Michigan	www.michigan.gov
Minnesota	www.governor.state.mn.us
Mississippi	www.mississippi.gov
Missouri	www.state.mo.us
Montana	www.state.mt.us
Nebraska	www.nebraska.gov
Nevada	www.nv.gov
New Hampshire	www.state.nh.us
New Jersey	www.state.nj.us
New Mexico	www.state.nm.us
New York	www.state.ny.us/
North Carolina	www.ncgov.com
North Dakota	http://discovernd.com
Ohio	www.state.oh.us
Oklahoma	www.youroklahoma.com
Rhode Island	www.state.ri.us
South Carolina	www.myscgov.com
South Dakota	www.state.sd.us
Tennessee	www.state.tn.us
Texas	www.state.tx.us
Utah	www.utah.go
Vermont	http://vermont.gov/

I have covered each of these laws in my book, *Become the Squeaky Wheel, a Credit and Collections Guide for Everyone.* You also can find them online.

ACCOUNTING SOFTWARE

When you start your business, you will open a checking account. You will want to decide if you want to use computer software to print your checks, do your billing, and reconcile your checkbook. There are many different types of accounting software out there but what I would recommend is, if you are hiring someone or going to use an accountant to do your taxes, ask them what they use and buy the same program or something that is compatible. When I hired my accountant, she told me what she used, and I went out and bought it. I use QuickBooks Pro Edition. This way, when I can't figure something out and call her office, someone there can help me right over the phone. Also, at the end of the year you can save your files to a disk and drop it off at the accountant's office and they can easily work on your files. This way you save money if they charge you by the hour, since they can just open it right up and it is the same program. They don't have to spend time trying to figure out a different program or trying to make it compatible with their system. You can visit any office supply store to see the different software options available to do your accounting and check their web sites for more information. Another way to choose your software, if you decide to do all this yourself, is to ask other business owners in your industry what they use—there might be a cus-

tomized program specific to your industry that will work better for you. If you join your local chamber, you can ask other members what they use and how they like it.

BILLING PROCEDURES

Setting up your billing and invoicing is as important as setting up your credit policy. This is what you send out in order to get paid. Some software allows you to e-mail the invoices to your customers, or you can print the invoices out and mail them. For the quickest payment, e-mailing or faxing the invoices works best; the customer has the invoice immediately. There is not the delay of mailing it, or the chance of it "getting lost in the mail" or lost on someone's desk. Also, if the customer becomes late, you can call and if they say they did not receive the bill or invoice, you can e-mail again or fax it immediately and call back to verify that they have it. Make sure you are not on their "spam" list or your e-mail will be blocked from getting through.

You should set up your billing to be done at the time of each sale rather than once a month. When work is completed, present your customer with an invoice immediately, whether it is in person, or by mail, fax, or e-mail. You also will want to choose a date, maybe the fifteenth of each month, to send out statements. Your accounting software can generate these for you as well and they also can be sent the same way. If you offer online payment, include that information on your billing and statements. The easier you make it for customers to pay, the better your chances of getting paid and getting paid on time.

MAINTAINING RECORDS

If you use an accounting software program, it will maintain a lot of your records for you if you do some easy data entry and keep up on it. For example, for bank statements you want to reconcile them with your software when you receive them. Your accounting software also should be able to print out a Profit and Loss at any time, or an Accounts Receivable or Payable aging any time. Using accounting software can automate much of your bookkeeping functions. If you don't have experience using them, you can check the web site for the software you choose and see if they have any training guides or materials. Also, many local schools and colleges will offer inexpensive classes one or two nights a week to teach the basics of common software most businesses use. The local university where I teach offers these classes online—this can be a good option if you don't have a lot of spare time.

CHAPTER 4

Invoicing and Statements

I F YOU HAVE PURCHASED QUICKBOOKS Pro or some other type of accounting software, you can use that to set up, print, and send your invoices and statements. Most programs will allow you to upload your logo and set up a template to match your needs for your business. For example, an invoice for a service business would be different from an invoice for a retail business. You can choose your fields, colors, address layout, and any special messages you want on your invoices and statements. You can usually customize quite a few different types, so you can use different styles for different services if you like. Remember that invoicing should be done immediately following the sale to ensure your cash flow will continue to flow consistently. Statements should be sent out monthly.

Either your invoices or statements or better yet, both, should include the following:

- Your address, URL, e-mail address, and toll-free number if you have one
- Your price, any discounts, and a final and total price
- Delivery specifications or directions; always include a phone number
- Your payment terms
- Your discount program in detail
- Any late fee or interest program in detail
- Notice that you will seek compensation for any debt-recovery costs if not paid

Tips to Faster Payments

- Make your invoices and statements look different from your receipts,

Take control!

If you don't set the payment terms for your business, your customers will.

letterhead, or quotes. A friend of mine prints her invoices on light-green paper and her statements on gold paper. I know before I open the envelope that it is a bill. If your letters, quotes, invoices, and statements all look alike it is more likely they will get lost or misplaced, and therefore not get paid on time or at all.

■ Make the total amount due stand out. I always make the total due on my invoices in a larger font and bold. You could underline or highlight the total due as well.

■ Tell your customers what you want them to do. PAY NOW or PAY IMMEDIATELY— you can type this into your billing program or buy a rubber stamp. If you purchase a stamp, try using red or blue ink.

■ Include pre-addressed and/or postage-paid payment envelopes.

■ Stamp an important message on the mailing envelope. You can use a rubber stamp or print right onto the envelopes. Some examples are:
  • Dated Material
  • As Requested
  • Confidential
  • Do Not Bend
  • Handle With Care
  • Personal

SETTING YOUR PAYMENT TERMS

If you don't set the payment terms for your business, your customers will. If there aren't any guidelines set up, the customer thinks it is not important to you, and will pay as they can or want. Be aware that this is not common knowledge. If you don't set up payment terms and call

a customer that hasn't paid you in 60 days, you can't expect to say, "Well, the law sets a default period of 'net 30 days'" and expect to have a lasting relationship or future orders from that customer. If no terms are set the law sets a default period of net 30 days. Your terms and conditions are the terms of the "contract" or "agreement" between you and your customers when they walk away from you having received something without giving you any money. The terms you set are to protect your rights, limit your liabilities, and provide you some security that you will get paid.

You will want to include your terms on your invoices, statements, and any contracts or agreements, and you can include it on the credit application. Some businesses print it on the back of their paperwork while others have it in small type along the bottom. This way you get your customer to agree to and acknowledge your terms of service and payment. Also, this is the time if you are giving a special discount, or extended payment terms, for you to change the terms and make a note of the new terms in their file.

If you do negotiate terms remember that the law allows you to challenge customers who try to impose terms and/or conditions upon you that remove your rights to claim late payment interest or compensation.

Here is an example of how your payment terms might look; this can be customized to fit your business.

Payment Terms

A. Payment terms are net thirty (30) days from date of invoice. Seller reserves the right to require alternative payment terms, including, without limitation, a letter of credit or payment in advance.

B. If payment is not received by the due date, a late charge will be added at the rate of one and one-half percent (1.5%) per month eighteen percent (18%) per year or the maximum legal rate, whichever is less, to unpaid invoices from the due date thereof.

C. All payments (checks) should be sent to:
Your Address
All payments by wire transfer should be submitted to:
Your bank name, address, and contact person

D. If buyer is delinquent in paying any amount owed to seller by more than ten (10) days, then without limiting any other rights and remedies available to seller under the law, in equity, or under the contract, seller may suspend production, shipment, and/or deliveries of any or all products purchased by buyer, or by notice to buyer, treat such delinquency as a repudiation by buyer of the portion of the contract not then fully performed, whereupon seller may cancel all further deliveries and any amounts unpaid hereunder shall immediately become due and payable. If seller retains a collection agency and/or attorney to collect overdue amounts, all collection costs, including attorney's fees and any court costs, shall be payable by buyer. Buyer hereby represents to seller that buyer is now solvent and agrees that each acceptance of delivery of the products sold hereunder shall constitute reaffirmation of this representation at such time.

Have a line after this statement for a signature and date on your new account forms and credit application.

CHARGING LATE FEES AND INTEREST

There are some things you should know before deciding on your late fees and interest charges. If you did not include any information about late fees or interest charges in your agreement or contract, or on any of your invoices or statements, you cannot add them on to a balance once the account is past due. A late fee also can be called a monthly finance charge. In order to charge the late fee you need to figure out what your monthly finance charge is. You can do this by dividing the annual interest rate you want to charge as a late fee by 12 to determine your monthly interest rate. Next, multiply this monthly interest rate by the amount due to determine the amount of the monthly late fee. Check with your state to find out the maximum amount you can charge for a late fee and then decide what you want to charge. Be sure to research your competition to see what they charge.

YOUR SMALL BUSINESS CAN GIVE DISCOUNTS!

No matter how small or new your business is, you can give a discount, even if you start out at 1 percent. Always show the total price then the discount with the new price under that. Some businesses also will add a line item that says something like: "You have saved $100." If the discount is substantial, that would be a good idea. When the discount is small, I would leave the total off and list the percentage, such as 5 percent or whatever the discount is. Offering a discount will show your customers that you appreciate their business and they will come back and refer you to others. Your discount has to be based on what you can afford. Look at this as an advertising expense, if you don't think you can afford it. When you are marketing your business, remember that it is 14 times harder to obtain a new customer than it is to have a repeat customer purchase from you again or refer you to someone else. You can justify this to yourself by knowing that this is part of your marketing strategy.

Before offering discounts, ask yourself:

- Can I afford to offer a discount and still make a profit?
- What will offering discounts do for my business?
- What discounts does my competition offer?

Offering your customer a discount can make them feel special and it creates loyalty. Maybe you want to offer a 10 percent discount to customers who spend a certain amount each month. Send them a special announcement when they qualify.

MAKING STATEMENTS WORK FOR YOUR SMALL BUSINESS

Quite a few small or new business owners don't even send out statements. They will just send out the invoices and then wait for payments. A monthly statement will show your clients that you are on top of your finances and keeping track of what is owed and what is paid. Larger customers or customers who are paying on account will be very appreciative of receiving their statements each month so they can see what they have paid and what their new balance is and any discounts or credits to their account.

My experience has been that business owners who do not send out statements have more requests from customers for invoice copies or a printout of their account, or something showing charges and payments made. This results in more work for you and your office staff, when you can instead send out statements easily with your accounting software. You can send them by e-mail to save postage, ink, and paper. It will show your customers you are professional and reliable.

OFFERING PAYMENT OPTIONS

The more options for payment for any of your services, the better your chances of making a sale and getting paid promptly. If you only do business on a cash basis, you miss out on a lot of good sales opportunities. There are many different options available for you to use. Some common forms of payment can be:

- Credit cards
- Debit cards
- Personal and business checks
- Online payments
- Money orders
- Cash

Pre-Payment Options

If you don't have a credit policy and don't want to extend credit to your customers, you can have them use a pre-payment option. This also could

VERIFY YOUR PAYMENTS!

Remember, you do not have to accept a check as a form of payment if you think it presents a risk.

Acceptance of a check as a form of payment is a privilege extended by you.

Cash and checks are *not* the same thing. When you accept a check you are crediting a customer with having sufficient funds in the bank to cover the check.

be combined with other forms of payment, such as credit cards, money orders, cash, or checks. If someone places an order you may want to have them pay up front—this could be a customer who had a bad credit history or who was denied for a credit account or maybe paid you with a bad or NSF check. They would be required to pay before the goods or services are provided. Make sure the payment "clears" before completing the transaction.

Checks

Most business owners accept checks as a form of payment. Remember, taking a check is a courtesy you extend to your customer. You are not obligated to take a check if you don't feel it is in your best interest. For example, some businesses will not accept a starter check from a new checking account or checks that are not imprinted with a name and address.

Following are some tips to help you avoid receiving bad checks.

The Do's of Check Acceptance

- Make sure name, address, and phone number are imprinted on the check.
- Use the current date only.
- Compare an ID picture with that of the person cashing or writing the check.
- Make sure the signature matches the ID signature.
- Make sure the phone number is a working phone.
- Ask for a street address—do not accept checks with imprinted post office box numbers.

The Don'ts of Check Acceptance

- Don't let the check writer rush you.
- Don't take any check, or person, for granted; *always* obtain proper ID.
- Don't accept pre-written personal checks. At least the signature should be written in your presence.
- Don't accept unsigned checks.
- Don't accept starter checks.
- Don't accept two-party checks.

When accepting a check, remember what is important:

- The check
- The identification
- The person

Spotting a Possible Problem Check

- Checks numbers under 300.
- Checks that do not have a phone number printed on them.
- If the address on the check is written by hand or if the current address is changed.

- Lack of photo ID.
- Checks drawn on out-of-state banks.
- Checks for more than the amount of purchase.
- Two-party checks.
- Check number handwritten, stamped, or typed.
- Loose checks not being recorded in a check register.

You don't have to accept a check as a form of payment if you think it presents a risk!

Spotting a Forged Check

- The check writer's name is different than the name printed on the check.
- The top or side of the check is smooth and not perforated.
- The bank numbers across the bottom appear glossy or irregular.
- Any difference or misalignment of type styles.
- Printing on the check appears faint or photocopied.
- Photo ID does not match information on the check.

You can accept checks by mail, over the phone, by fax, or online. Check with your bank to see if they offer any program you can use, or visit www.checkman.com. You can order special checks from them and print the checks for deposit into your bank account. They also offer a web form for your web site, with instructions for customers on where to find the checking account information that you will need to process the check. Visit checkman.com for more information, testimonials, and resources. You also can do a search online for other companies that offer this service.

When you receive a call or notice from your bank that a check has been returned for NSF, call the bank the check is drawn on to see if it will clear. If so, re-deposit it, if not pick up the phone and call that customer immediately. Tell them you are depositing the check again tomorrow and that they need to make sure the funds are there. If you charge an NSF fee, tell them how much that is, and ask them to come in and pay that now. If they are not a local account, take a credit card payment or tell them to mail that fee today. Put the account on hold until the check and all fees are paid. If the check comes back a second time, call the customer and revoke their credit limit.

Credit Cards

Accepting credit or debit cards is so common these days that it is unusual if you don't accept them. They are easy to set up—you should check with the bank you have your business account with, and set up a merchant account. Once you are set up, the money will be automatically deposited into your checking account from any charges you process. You have a few options when accepting credit cards—if you are a store front you might want to have the box where you swipe the card. You also can purchase or download software to process the credit or debit card payments with your computer or cash register. You also can run them by calling a toll-free number and using your key pad on your phone to send the information. When you are setting up your merchant account, you will be asked you how you want to process the charges. You will get a monthly statement from your merchant account just as you do from your bank for your checking account. The payments and fees will be broken down by Visa, MasterCard, and Discover, or any other credit cards you accept.

If you send out statements by e-mail with a link to a payment page on your web site that customers can just click on and input their debit or credit card information to pay your bill, you will get a lot more payments quicker. The more convenient you make it for your customers to pay you, the more you will get paid on time and in full.

Online Payments

Taking online payments will boost your cash flow immensely. A lot of people pay their bills at night or on weekends. If you offer online payment options, those are available to your customers 24/7. They can pay you anytime, day or night. Customers love this option—it lets them be in control and pay at their leisure, almost effortlessly. You should have a secure payment page on your web site. For example, the prefix of your URL would change from *http* to *https*, with the *s* meaning secure. You can purchase a secure certificate at https://www.thawte.com/; the SSL Web Server Certificate offers comprehensive authentication procedures (domain name and identity

verification). It also offers 256-, 128-, 56-, or 40-bit encryption depending on your clients' browser's capability and the cipher suite installed on your web server. This ensures that information is kept private while in transit between your web server and your clients' web browsers.

Automatic Bill Pay

If you set up your customers with an automatic bill paying system, you will need written and signed authorization. You can set this up to charge a checking account or a debit or credit card. I have included a sample form for your reference.

You also may customize the form for a credit or debit card automatic monthly payment. Always be very specific and have your customer sign the form. Keep it with your customer's file. If you will be charging any fees if the payment is declined, or if you have a policy about denied automatic payments, print them on this form. Maybe you want to let them know that your policy is that you will try a card or deposit a check twice, but after that the balance is due and will accrue a late charge or interest if not paid by some other means. You may accept a faxed copy of this form but an original signature is always

Automatic Bill Pay Authorization Form for Checks/Checking Accounts

---

Your Company Name

Date

Your Customer's Name and Address

Dear

By signing and returning this form, you are giving permission to YOUR COMPANY NAME to print one or more drafts as listed below to be drawn against the following account(s):

Bank name	Bank transit numbers	Check number

Such drafts will be used as payments toward your account(s) listed with YOUR COMPANY NAME.

Your current balance of all accounts listed is $100.00.

Please sign and date this form and return to:

COMPANY NAME AND ADDRESS

Draft date	Draft number	Draft amount

Signature _____   Date_____

Remember to void these checks in your checkbook, and enter the amounts and dates into your check register.

Sincerely,

Your company name

Your name
Your title

---

better.

Credit Card Authorization Form

Account #: _____   Date: _____

Company Name: _____

Address: _____

_____

Phone: _____

Cardholder's Name: _____

Type of Card: MASTER CARD   VISA   AM EX   DISCOVER

Card Number: _____

Exp. Date: _____

I hereby authorize (your company name) to automatically charge the above credit card whenever I place an order with them, unless there is a prior written notice.

Signature of cardholder: _____

Date: _____

PART II

Components of a
Credit Policy

CHAPTER 5

What Is a Credit Policy?

MAKE YOUR CREDIT POLICY SHORT, easy, and to the point. Watch for changes in the economy and don't create such a detailed policy that you can't handle it.

There are specific components or parts of a credit policy. Some things to remember when you are creating your credit policy are the various things that can affect your policy or make it different from that of another company. Business owners all have different types of businesses but can all extend credit. So it should only make sense that no two credit policies will be the same. One major difference is if you have a service or retail business. Your credit policy should use multiple facets to cater to prospective customers but also protect you, the business owner.

You are limited in what you can and can't ask a prospective customer in order to extend them credit. Business owners

need to be aware of what these questions are and what the laws are before they create their credit policy. Your credit policy helps to filter customers so you don't have to spend your time chasing your money. Your best policy will be short, easy, and to the point; it will avoid long-winded statements and a lot of "legalese" or big words. Always create your forms with the reader in mind—the easier and clearer the better.

One component to be aware of is local and/or national unemployment figures. Keep your eye on the economy. If a large company in your local area goes out of business, your customers who worked there will be out of work and may be unable to pay their bills, yours included.

When you create your credit policy make sure you create something you can easily maintain. Credit can be a full-time job. If you're a sole proprietor and only have time to do parts of a policy, figure out what will be the most effective and realistic for you to maintain. If you create a policy you can't maintain you will become frustrated and lose money. Having a credit policy and not being able to maintain it will only hurt your business and cause you stress.

WHY YOUR SMALL BUSINESS NEEDS A CREDIT POLICY

Some business owners ask, "Why do I need a credit policy? I don't have much bad debt." The following will help you to understand and decide if you want or need to implement a credit policy. It is my belief that every business should have a credit policy and that any bad debt is too much.

A credit policy should:

- Provide timely notification to customers regarding past due amounts, and therefore eliminate old balances from being carried on your receivables
- Outline a procedure that will provide customers with options when they cannot pay in full or on time, or if they want to make a large purchase
- Provide a procedure on when and what to do with small balances on customers' accounts
- Provide a procedure that will enable a company to adequately provide reasonable credit limits for customers with revolving credit
- Provide guidelines to legally collect money owed to your company that was lost due to bad checks
- Provide you with a system that will maintain timely contact with customers when they are past due

- Provide a procedure that will enable your business to keep credit card numbers and checking account information on file for customers and automatically charge them when they place an order or for scheduled monthly or weekly payments
- Enable your business to be aware of when an account should be placed for collection and to avoid carrying bad debts on the receivables or your books
- Provide you with a procedure that will eliminate orders being held for nonpayment and to better serve customers in a timely manner
- Enable you to be aware of when to write off a balance to bad debt

It is not just important for you to understand your credit policy, it is also very important for your customers and employees to understand it as well. It is your job to educate your customers and employees on your credit policy in order for it to work well for you, your business, and your customers. It is important that your customers know your credit policy and/or terms of payment before they ever start doing business with you. Reiteration of your credit policy, every chance you get, is a good business practice to get into. You can do this many ways; you can include information about your credit policy on the back of your invoices and statements. You should give every new customer a copy of your credit guidelines when they fill out a credit application. This can be a separate sheet or printed on the back of the credit application. Having your customer sign that they understand your credit policies will help you down the line if payment becomes late or is not received.

> The human species, according to the best theory I can form of it, is composed of two distinct races, the men who borrow and the men who lend.
>
> —Charles Lamb
> The Two Races of Men in *Essays of Elia*, 1823

There are many reasons why you should implement a credit policy, most importantly for you and your customers. You want to protect yourself against bad debt and also portray to potential customers that you are a professional. Your credit policy should benefit you, the business owner, and also your customers. You should consider your credit policy a form of customer service that you are offering your potential and existing clients. You could easily only accept payment upon receipt of your product or service. A credit policy is not something that should scare your customers away—you can become more profitable and have a smoother running business if you create a credit policy that will streamline your billing, new customers account setup, and payments. Your customers will appreciate knowing your payment guidelines, how and when they can pay, and the ease of automatic billing. This will result in happy customers who make more purchases if they can pay later, and more sales, success, and money for you, the business owner.

A credit policy can be easily implemented and can be as detailed as you like. Some objectives you should consider when implementing your credit policy are to provide timely notification to customers regarding their balances, any discounts offered, and past due amounts, therefore eliminating old balances from being carried on the receivables. Your policy will outline a procedure that will provide your customers with options when they cannot pay in full or on time. Or maybe they wish to make a large purchase and pay on account; your policy should outline the payment terms of that account or transaction. You want your credit policy to provide procedures that will enable your company to adequately provide reasonable credit limits for customers customers to whom you offer revolving credit accounts, and a system that outlines how to decide who gets a revolving credit account and how much credit you wish to extend to them. Studies show that customers who have the option to pay later will normally make a larger purchase.

A very important aspect of your credit policy is to provide legal guidelines to collect money due your company that is lost due to bad checks or nonpayment of accounts. Creditors need to be aware of state and federal laws when doing any type of debt collection. You or your credit manager need to be familiar with these laws or use a collection service that is familiar with them. The laws you need to be familiar with are the Fair Debt Collection Practices Act and also any specific laws in your state or the states in which you do business.

Your credit policy should:

- Outline your inhouse procedures on setting up new accounts and determining credit limits
- Use a system that will maintain timely contact with customers when they are past due

- Provide a procedure that will enable your company to use automatic billing or payments
- Help you determine how and when to send dunning notices
- Help you determine when to place an account with an outside collection agency
- Help you determine when to write off a debt to bad debt
- Help you to better serve your customers and keep them coming back

Your company is not protected from bad debt, so you need to protect yourself by:

- Having a sound credit policy and sticking to it
- Getting a signed credit application
- Checking references
- Getting a signed contract or agreement
- Pulling a credit report if possible
- Setting a reasonable credit limit
- Staying on top of your customers' accounts and balances

Adhere to your credit policy no matter what. Make sure your staff, especially your sales force, knows they cannot make changes or authorize "special terms." My experience has been that the sales department is the hardest to train to adhere to a credit policy. They want to make the sale, so they will try to bend the rules. I always offered that they put the blame on me or the credit department. You will still get requests for different terms and can make that decision based on the information the salesperson provides for that customer. You cannot see the future or change market conditions. Try to keep current with trade reports pertaining to specific companies and industries. There are many free reports available as well as paid subscriptions. Some things you can do to keep payments flowing smoothly are:

- Change your collection letters frequently; you can make them stronger and more action oriented.
- Discourage payments on account or changes in payment terms. Too many payment plans or changed payment terms can impair your cash flow.
- When you receive unauthorized or authorized "payments on account," be sure to follow up right away with a letter or phone call thanking the customer for their payment and telling them the new balance, where and when to send the next payment, and if possible, send them a payment envelope. Tell them to send the balance immediately. Remember to tell them what to do—"Pay Now."
- On larger accounts call or send a reminder just a few days after terms if they get delinquent.
- Ask to speak to a manager or owner when making collection calls, rather than speaking to a "gatekeeper" or secretary. Go right for the decision maker.
- If a customer disputes the quality of merchandise or service, price, or delivery, you should attempt to resolve this immediately. Insist that they pay the portion of the bill that they are not disputing while you work on the disputed portion.
- If all else fails, you may want to refer the account to an outside collection agency.

A common question I am asked by new business owners is, "What if I don't have the time or the money to hire a credit manager but want to avoid bad debt?" If you do only one thing to make your cash flow better, do this! If you do not implement a credit policy, one thing you can do right away to help make your business more money and have less bad debt, is to have every potential customer fill out a credit application. You can make your own, buy them at an office supply store, or download one for free at www.credit-and-collections.com. Keep these on your front counter or mail them to anyone who calls. You should also have one on your web site for immediate download. Be sure to have the customer sign it and give them a copy. Once you have the credit application, check the references and keep the application in a locked file cabinet. Even if you let this person get out of control with payments, once you place the account with a collection agency, just having the credit application makes their job easier, which makes your chances of getting your money much better.

If you are creating your own credit application, educate yourself on what you can and cannot ask a potential customer. Obtain the following information from a business and/or consumer seeking credit:

- Business and owner's name
- Length they have been in business
- Address, length of time at that address, and a former address
- Balance sheets or IRS returns
- Phone numbers of business and principals and residence
- Bank name, address, and phone number
- Credit references, personal and business
- Employer name, address, and phone number

- Length of time at current employment
- Marital status, name, and employment information on spouse
- Total monthly household income
- Social security number and/or federal ID number

Also remember, successful businesses have a credit policy in place and enforce it. Nobody likes to work for free. Remember one of the key reasons you want a credit policy is so that you control your money. Don't let your customers control the success of your business.

Potential and existing customers will know you are serious if:

- They have to fill out a credit application.
- They have to sign a contract or agreement.
- They receive invoices right away.
- You *send* your invoices right away, as soon as items have shipped or the work is complete, either by mail, e-mail, or fax.
- You call right away if you don't receive payment. Don't wait!
- You gather all the information you can about the customer before making a sale.
- You are professional at all times.
- You are persistent.
- You make personal visits when you can.
- You offer different payment options.
- You charge a late fee or finance charge.

If you do not create or implement a credit policy, your customers do not have any guidelines for payment and therefore will pay as they like, creating a very lenient credit policy. Once this happens it is very hard to "re-train" customers to adhere to a stricter credit policy. Do not make this mistake.

Instead of giving your customers or potential customers a choice between you and your competition and having them choose the other guy, have them choose you.

Some customers, when given the choice between signing a credit application or paying at the time of sale, mostly choose the credit application regardless of who has the cheaper prices. It is true that some customers will buy more from you if they are approved for credit and have more time to pay. It makes it easy for them to place orders and receive a bill, rather than have to pay at the point of sale.

Like everything else, the easier you make it for the customer to buy from you the more sales you will have. Customers want things to be easy, fast, and instant. If they are credit-approved and can call, order, and have the item quickly then pay when they receive a bill, they will be more likely to order from you than someone who doesn't offer that option. They also will be more likely to order more since they can pay later, resulting in your business making more money and more sales.

Your business needs a credit policy so you or your office staff know when to write off accounts to bad debt, when to put past due accounts on hold or bring them to your attention for more action, when to send dunning letters or notices, when it is acceptable to set up a payment plan and what those payments should be, and the frequency of the payments in order to maintain cash flow to your business. Other reasons you need a credit policy include knowing how to handle a returned check, how and when to make collection calls, how to follow up on calls and letters, when to use an outside collection agency, and

how to choose one that will work well for your business.

Your credit policy ensures you have a steady cash flow in your business, which determines if you will pay your bills on time and be successful. If you already have a business and do not have a credit policy, implementing a credit policy and enforcing it can increase your cash flow dramatically, resulting in your having more money and better paying customers, and growing your business successfully.

HOW A CREDIT POLICY AFFECTS YOUR CUSTOMERS

Your credit policy is a two-way street—you create the rules and your customers have to play by them, since this is your game. If your customers don't follow your rules, they are out of the game. It is up to you to be fair, reasonable, and follow the law to ensure your customers will not be intimidated by your credit policy and will continue to be good paying customers who refer you to others.

Some customers with bad credit look for businesses they can order from without having to fill out a credit application or any type of new account forms. If a customer balks at filling out any new account information, set them up as COD or pre-payment only. Never extend credit without getting at least a signed credit application and checking references.

A good customer will not run away when they have to fill out any paperwork, and will be glad they are dealing with an organized, professional business. They will feel more secure doing business with you and know you are serious about your business. This elevates your business in the eyes of customers—they will know you are an upstanding business owner with values and they will want to do business with you and refer you to their friends.

When a potential customer fills out a credit application you can get near-perfect information about that customer and how they pay their bills, and if they can afford more debt. Most consumers who take the time to fill out a credit application are serious about buying from you; otherwise they would just go down the road to where they can buy without filling out any forms.

After extensive research it was found that consumers who can obtain credit will even pay more for a product or service when they are extended credit and have great customer service. The faster, easier, and smoother procedures will get the most and better-paying customers. The result is more sales, more income, and happier customers for your business. This also can result in word-of-mouth advertising from happy customers, and that is free.

SETTING PROCEDURES

It is important that your customers know your credit policy and payment terms before they even begin doing business with you. Reiteration of your credit policy and procedures when payment is overdue is a good step to take in trying to obtain payment. Always ask for payment when it is justly due.

You should never extend credit to a new customer without having them fill out a credit application and go through the credit approval policy. Once you extend credit, it is important to maintain accurate records on an accounts' payment history.

Adhere to your collection policies no matter what may transpire. You cannot see the future or changing market conditions. Try to keep current with trade reports pertaining to specific companies and industries. You can try Eli Financials Debt Collection Compliance Alert Newsletter, a paid subscription, however, if you join my Credit and Collections Group, www.credit-and-collections.com, you can get a discounted rate. You can get many special deals on industry trends magazines and newsletters when you join my networking group. My group and web site will teach you techniques to help you in your collection efforts and in setting up procedures to help you increase your credit department's efficiency.

Procedures should be in writing and everyone in your employ should have a copy as well as your customers. You also can frame a copy and hang it in your lobby or waiting room. An easy way to set up your procedures is with a simple checklist. Use the checklist to create "new account" packets and leave them in your front office or at the front desk for new customers to take and fill out. These packets should include the following:

1. Credit application
2. Credit policy (may be printed on the back of the credit application)
3. Forms for automatic payments by check or credit card
4. Reference sheet if not included on your credit application

You can print out these forms and clip them together or put them in a clipboard and hand them to every new customer to fill out. Make it a habit of yours and your employees and you should never make an exception. If you have a web site you can include this information as a free download for customers to complete and send back to you.

Some steps you can take to make your credit policy easy, quick, and painless are:

1. Make it easy for the customer to get credit with you. Have packets paper-clipped together at the front desk; include the credit application, automatic payment permission forms, and anything else you want filled out before opening an account.

2. Make it quick, by having these packets ready and waiting for anyone who comes in. Have pens and clipboards available so they can be filled out immediately.

3. Make it painless, by either having them wait and running the credit application while they are still there or responding to them within a certain time period, say 24 hours.

Consumers today, like everyone else, expect convenience and speed. If you make opening up a credit account difficult or are unorganized, you can lose the customer.

Customers who are approved for credit will buy more if they can pay later, so make the process as streamlined as you can. Another option is to advertise a free gift. You know how banks offer a free toaster or blanket when you open a new checking account? Try offering something, maybe a discount for credit-approved customers in a certain time frame. For example, "Get 25 percent off your first order if you apply for a credit account and are credit-approved between January 1 and January 14, 2007." You also could offer this type of deal to existing customers.

Advertise that if they refer someone who becomes a credit-approved customer and places an order for $50 or more, you will give them 5 percent off their next order.

FORMS, LETTERS, AND APPLICATIONS

The most effective letters are short and sweet, to the point, and easy to read. Try to stay away from long or confusing words and sentences. The more direct a letter is, the less misunderstandings are possible. Have someone read your letter and see if they fully understand it. If they do, then chances are your debtor will as well.

Your letter is a reflection of your business, keep it professional. Remember that your letter is to persuade someone to send you money. Your wording and tone are critical, especially if this is a customer you want to continue to do business with. Always assume the debtor will pay—enclosing an envelope for payment is always a good idea. The easier you make it for the debtor to make a payment, the better your chances of receiving that payment are.

New Account Forms

You can create your own forms, letters, and applications or purchase them at an office supply store. You also can buy books of letters and forms, I have a few books of just letters and forms you can use on my web site at www.michelledunn.com. These books include every kind of form, application, and letter you might need to run your business efficiently. I also have included some in this book. A new account form can also be a credit application. It might be an informational form so you can learn about your customer and their needs. You

Request for References

Date _____

Name _____

Mailing Address _____

_____

Legal Business Name (if applicable) _____

Phone _____ Fax _____ E-mail _____

Manner of Payment _____

Discounts _____

Prompt _____ Slow _____

How Many Days _____

COD Account _____

Customer Since _____

High Credit $_____ Amount Now Owing $_____

Past Due Amount $_____ Terms _____

Comments _____

_____

Banks _____

Name _____

Address _____

_____

Phone _____ Fax _____ E-mail _____

Average Checking Account Balance $_____

NSF Checks $_____

Loan Experiences _____

Customer Since _____

Security Held _____

Comments _____

_____

might ask how they heard of you, if they want to be added to your mailing list, and other information to help you serve your customers or help you with your marketing efforts. Appendix A includes an example of a new account form.

Credit Denied or Accepted Letters

If you pull credit reports, you will need to send your customers a letter letting them know if the application was denied or approved. A Credit Denied Letter (page 51) should include the information in the example but can be customized to your business.

The same scenario applies if you approve a new customer for credit—you need to send them a letter letting them know they have been approved and how much their credit limit is. On page 52 is a sample Credit Approved Letter.

You can and should customize the approval letter with your payment terms and conditions, any information about your late fees and discounts, and a notice that it is your practice to send out monthly statements.

Credit Applications

The best way to get credit information is to have a customer fill out a credit application. I have included a sample Credit Application that you can use or modify to suit your business. I also have some free Credit Applications at www.credit-and-collections.com that you can download and modify. The main reason you will want to use a credit application is to gather the credit information that you can check to decide if you want to extend credit. You may also use the credit application to help you collect on the

account if it ever becomes past due. You can use the same credit application for consumer or business accounts or use different applications as you wish.

What will a credit application do for me and my business?

- A credit application provides you with customer credit worthiness.
- A credit application provides you with the best opportunity (before a sale is made) to find out something you may need to know down the road. Most customers are willing to give you all the information you need before the sale because they want credit from you.

On your credit application you will want to have a statement such as:

- "The undersigned hereby agrees that should a credit account be opened, and in the event of default in the payment of any amount due, and if such account is submitted to a collection authority, customer will be required to pay an additional charge equal to the cost of collection including court costs."
- "The undersigned individual who is either a principal of the credit applicant or a sole proprietorship of the credit applicant, recognizing that his or her individual credit history may be a factor in the evaluation of the credit history of the applicant, hereby consents to and authorizes the use of a consumer credit report on the undersigned by the above named business credit grantor, from time to time as may be needed, in the credit evaluation process."

Prospective Applicant Denial Letter

Date

Dear

Your application for credit with YOUR COMPANY NAME has unfortunately been denied.

One or more of the reasons for the denial of your application may be found in:

❏ Information contained in a consumer credit report obtained from: (See List Below)

❏ A consumer credit report containing information insufficient to our need was obtained from: (See List Below)

❏ The fact that the consumer reporting agency contacted was unable to supply any information about you. (See List Below)

❏ Information was received from a person or company other than a consumer reporting agency. You have a right to make a written request within 60 days of receiving this letter for a disclosure of the nature of this information. Pursuant to federal law, we are prohibited from disclosing the source of this information.

When a credit report is used in making the decision, the Fair Credit Reporting Act requires us to tell you where we obtained that report.

That company may also have obtained information on you from one or more of the consumer reporting agencies whose names, addresses, and phone numbers are listed below. They and the other agencies only provide information about your credit history. They took no part in making the decision, nor can they explain why this decision was made.

The following (checked) consumer reporting agencies supplied your credit information:

❏ Experian (TRW) Consumer Assistance, P.O. Box 949, Allen, TX 75002 (800) 682-7654

❏ TransUnion Consumer Relations, P.O. Box 1000, 2 Baldwin Place, Chester, PA 19022 (800) 888-4213

❏ CBI/Equifax Credit Information Services, P.O. Box 740241, Atlanta, GA 30374-2041 (800) 685-1111

You have certain rights under federal law to get a copy of your report, dispute its accuracy, and insert a consumer statement. If you believe your file contains errors, is inaccurate, or is incomplete call the consumer reporting agency that has been checked at their toll-free number, or write to them using the information listed above for disclosure. The disclosure can be made orally, in writing, or electronically. You also have a right during the 60-day period that starts DATE to receive a free copy of your consumer report from the consumer reporting agency whose name is checked off above.

You have a right to dispute the accuracy or completeness of any information contained in your consumer credit report, as furnished by the consumer reporting agency whose name is checked off above.

Prospective Applicant Denial Letter (continued)

> You have the right to put into your file a consumer statement up to 100 words in length to explain items in your file.
>
> Customer assistance at the credit reporting agency whose name has been checked is available to help you with the consumer statement.
>
> You may have additional rights under the credit reporting or consumer protection laws of your state. If you wish, you may contact your state or local consumer protection agency or a state Attorney General's office.
>
> Thank you for your application. I wish you the best in your future endeavors.
>
> Sincerely,

Credit Approved Letter

> Date
>
> Name and Address
>
> Dear
>
> Thank you for applying for credit with YOUR COMPANY NAME. We are happy to inform you that your account has been approved and your credit limit is $5,000.00.
>
> Please refer to the back of this notice for our terms and conditions for payment.
>
> Sincerely,

- "My signature indicates that I understand and agree to comply fully with the terms and conditions enumerated in this credit application." (You would want to use this if you have included your credit terms on the application.)
- "My signature certifies that everything I have stated in the application is correct to the best of my knowledge."

If you decide to create your own credit applications, consult with your attorney since there are certain questions that credit granters are not allowed to ask consumers. For example, you are not permitted to ask a credit applicant about his or her marital status, unless the account will be a joint account. You cannot deny credit based on marital status. Applicants do not have to tell you if they receive income from welfare, child support, or alimony. You cannot discriminate against applicants on the basis of sex, marital status, race, color, religion, national origin, or age.

If your application is geared more toward businesses rather than consumers you will want to ask questions on the following topics.

- The company's legal name—it should be officially registered with the state in which the company does business
- All names, addresses, and social security numbers of the principals of the company
- The company's address, length of time there, and the previous address, if they have been there less than one year
- How many years the company has been in business
- The company's bank name, address, type of account(s), and account number(s)
- Three or four trade references
- The type of service or product the company supplies
- Federal ID number

You might also want to include a personal guarantee on a business account. This way, an office or owner of a company could be held personally responsible for any business debts.

You also will want to update your credit application that you have on file, maybe once or twice a year depending on your business. If you think a company may be in financial trouble you might want to update the credit application quarterly.

In some cases you may allow a co-signer on the application. If you do, you must get the same information as you have for the main contact. Check all references and if you do approve credit and the main contact defaults, you would go after the co-signer for your money. When approving a co-signer remember that co-signers should be able to pay back the loan as if it were their own. Studies show that for co-signed credit or loans that go unpaid by the original customer, three to four co-signers are asked to repay the loan.

The credit application is important when starting a relationship with a new customer. This form will help you to decide what credit limit to extend, and if a bill is not paid, it will help you to collect your money. You should be looking for stable income or employment, someone who does not have a lot of debt, good existing credit, and no NSF checks, judgments, or collection accounts.

If you pull a credit report on the person who has filled out the credit application, here are some things to look for when deciding whether to approve them for credit:

- Have they paid their bills on time?
- What is their outstanding debt?
- How long is their credit history?
- How long have they been at their current job and address?
- Have they applied for new credit recently, with whom and how often?
- What types of credit accounts do they currently have and how many?
- Are their accounts current?

Some specific questions to ask a business that has filled out a credit application are:
- Ask them to list their 3 major suppliers
  - Name
  - Contact person
  - Phone/e-mail/fax
  - Billing and delivery addresses

- List 3 other suppliers, such as office products, or cleaning supplies
- Ask for the name of a supplier who has denied them credit
- Ask for the reason they are "switching" or "adding" you to their vendors. If you are replacing a supplier, ask why.

RESULTS OF A CREDIT POLICY

Once you have a credit policy in place you will know how to maintain your cash flow to benefit you and your business. You will know how to get customers to pay easily and quickly. The longer you don't do anything about getting paid, the chances you will get paid are much less. Having a credit policy helps you, the business owner, to keep your customers happy and get paid. Having a credit and collections policy sets a positive credit tone for your business. It also lets potential customers know that you mean business. It puts you in control of your customers, cash flow, and profits.

It is up to you how tight a ship you want to run. You can have a very tight credit policy, at the risk of alienating customers, or a very loose one if you are willing to take a bigger risk. Some business owners have looser credit policies for a variety of reasons. They may want to open several new accounts quickly and don't mind taking the risk. They may be in a big city and in a competitive industry or they may offer looser credit terms for a limited time to introduce a new service or product. They may have a large inventory in a warehouse and want to move it quickly.

TOP FOUR COLLECTION MISTAKES

You've got hundreds of new customers. Great! Are they paying you on time? If not, you need to "become the squeaky wheel." Make sure you aren't making any of the following common collection mistakes:

1. No credit policy in place—When you started your business you had a business plan and you use a marketing plan to publicize your business. Do yourself a favor and create a credit policy so you can have a financial plan. *Become the Squeaky Wheel*, by Michelle Dunn, gives you the tools you need to create a credit policy.

2. Extending credit to anyone—When you go to buy a new riding lawnmower, or washer and dryer, and can't afford to pay all at once, you always have to fill out paperwork. Are you extending credit to customers without having them sign or fill out a credit application? Download a free credit application at www.credit-and-collections.com or order *How to Help You Get Paid*, by Michelle Dunn, for more sample applications.

3. Not using a credit policy to make more money and more sales—When you don't have a credit policy in place, you will probably have a lot of customers, but how many are paying in full and on time and how many are placing repeat or large orders? When you implement a credit policy, you create a solid customer base of good paying customers with credit limits that allow them to make larger and more frequent purchases.

4. Receiving too many NSF notices or bad checks—Are you getting checks returned to you for NSF? Do you accept checks from any customer without verifying their information or checking ID? Accepting a check as a form of payment is a privilege you extend to your customer based on the unspoken promise that there are sufficient funds to cover the check.

Now look at your business with an unbiased eye. Do you have customers who owe you money? Do you have a credit policy in place? Do you want to get paid in full and on time and make more sales and money? Creating a credit policy can be as easy as having a completed and signed credit application.

CHAPTER 6

What Is Credit Risk?

CREDIT RISK IS THE RISK OF LOSS DUE TO A default on a contract, or more generally, the risk of loss due to some "credit event." Traditionally, this only applied to situations where debt holders or business owners were concerned that the debtor or customer to whom they made a loan or extended credit might default on a payment. For that reason, credit risk is sometimes also called *default risk*.

In business, almost all companies carry some credit risk, because most companies do not demand up-front cash payments for all products delivered and services rendered. Instead, most companies deliver the product or service, and then bill the customer, often specifying their terms of payment. Credit risk is the time in between when the customer leaves with the product or service and when you get paid.

MANAGING CREDIT RISK

Managing credit risk is important for any business but especially for new or small businesses. For large companies, there may be a credit risk department whose job it is to assess the financial health of their customers and extend credit (or not) accordingly, much like a credit manager. For example, a new business that is selling its products to a troubled customer may attempt to lessen credit risk by tightening payment terms to "net 15," or by actually selling less product on credit to the retailer, or even cutting off credit entirely, and demanding payment in advance. They might even lower the credit limit they have established and re-run the credit report to re-evaluate the credit risk situation. This will probably cause friction in the relationship with the customer, but you will end up better off if the customer is late paying their bills, or, especially, if they default and you have to place the account for collection, take them to court, or if they file bankruptcy.

Credit risk is not really manageable for very small companies (i.e., those with only one or two customers). This makes these companies very vulnerable to defaults or even payment delays by their customers. Thus the reason to have a sound credit policy in place.

CHECKING CREDIT

Once you have a new customer and they want to apply for credit, you have to check their credit in order to make an educated decision on how much credit you want to extend to them, or how much of a risk you want to take by how much credit you extend to them. If you have signed up with a credit reporting agency to pull credit reports, you want to run a credit report once you have the signed credit application back in your office. You also will want to check all references. Remember, most people put down references that they know are good, but check them all anyway. Make notes right on the credit application or new account form. Call the business references, personal references, and their banks. Always get the full name, title, and extension of the person giving the reference.

> Why do I have to spend money to check credit?
>
> The cost to run a credit report through a credit bureau or credit reporting agency is an investment that is well worth it.

Some questions you can ask are:

- How long have you known the customer?
- How long has the customer been doing business with you?
- What payment method does the customer normally use?
- Does the customer pay within terms, late, or early to take a discount?
- What is the customer's average balance and how many days past due?
- What is the average amount of the customer's orders?
- How often does the customer order from you?
- What is the customer's current balance due? Is any of that past due? If yes, how many days past due?
- What are the customer's terms with you?
- Does the customer make a lot of returns?
- Does the customer take any discounts?
- What is the customer's high credit in the last year or six months? (*High credit* is the most money they have owed at one time.)
- Is the customer's account current today or now?

When you contact the bank for a reference, you sometimes will have to fax your request on your company letterhead stating that you have authorization from the customer to request the credit reference information. You can easily type this up on your letterhead and fax it, then call right back.

Things to ask the bank:

- What type of account do they have? Business, personal, savings, checking?
- When did they open the account?

- What is their average daily balance?
- Have they had any NSF or other returned checks?
- Do they have any outstanding loans?
- What types of loans do they have?
- Are the loans secured or unsecured?
- Are they being paid as agreed?

Many new or small business owners or credit managers balk at running a credit report because there is a cost. Depending on what you pay, think of this amount in relation to what you could lose by not pulling the report and checking their credit. The cost to run a credit report is an investment that is well worth it.

> You cannot deny credit based on race, sex, marital status, religion, age, national origin, or receipt of public assistance.

HOW TO RUN AND READ CREDIT REPORTS

When you sign up with one or all three of the credit bureaus you can sign up to run credit reports. Some of the bureaus allow you to do this online through their web sites, or you can download a program and print the reports on your office printer. They also will have someone who will be able to educate you on how to read the credit reports and what all the fields mean. You also can check their web sites for tutorials on how to do this. An explanation usually accompanies any report you receive. It describes legal rights and other helpful information. You can also always call the credit bureau that you sign up with and who supplied you with the report for an explanation.

Credit histories come from public records or organizations that have granted credit to someone. An asterisk by an account indicates that the item may require further review by a prospective creditor when checking the credit history.

To pull or run a credit report you must have a permissible purpose. The federal Fair Credit Reporting Act (FCRA) requires that a notice be provided to inform users of consumer reports of their legal obligations. State law may impose additional requirements. This first section of the summary sets forth the responsibilities imposed by the FCRA on any users of consumer reports. The subsequent sections of the Act discuss the duties of users or reports that contain specific types of information or that are used for certain purposes, and the legal consequences of violations. The FCRA, 15 U.S.C. 1681-168lu, is set forth in full at the Federal Trade Commission's Internet web site at www.ftc.gov.

Things the FCRA covers:

- Obligations of all users of consumer reports
- Reuirement that users must provide certifications
- Requirements that sers must notify consumers when adverse actions are taken
- Obligations of users when consumer reports are obtained for employment purposes
- Obligations of users of investigative consumer reports
- Obligations of users of consumer reports containing medical information

- Obligations of users of "prescreened" lists
- Obligations of resellers
- Liability for violations of the FCRA

WHAT IS ON A CREDIT REPORT?

- Name
- Alias or aka (also known as)
- Current and previous addresses
- Social Security numbers
- Telephone numbers
- Date of birth
- Current and previous employers
- Credit history
- Retail stores
- Banks
- Finance companies
- Mortgage companies
- Public records
- Tax liens
- Court judgments (including child support judgments)
- Bankruptcies
- Inquiries made
- Credit grantors and other authorized parties who have requested a copy of the consumer's credit report with a legally permissible purpose.
- Credit grantors with whom a consumer has an existing relationship and who are permitted to periodically review the information. If you review accounts twice a year or once a year, this will show up here.
- Companies, with a legally permissible purpose, that have obtained certain limited information about a consumer, such as name and address, in order to send tar-

geted, mutually beneficial firm offers of credit or insurance.

- Some of the bureaus also offer, at a business's request, additional features such as a model profile section, a credit summary, or special messages on potentially fraudulent or invalid information. In addition, any consumer statements and other Fair Credit Reporting Act information will be displayed.

Did you know...?

- Reported collection accounts stay on someone's credit report for seven years.
- Judgments stay on a credit report seven years from the filing date, except for bankruptcy records.
- Bankruptcy records stay on a report ten years from the filing date. This includes Chapter 7, Chapter 11, and Chapter 13.
- Credit inquiries stay on a report for two years. This would be when you pull a report for employment or to check credit.

CREDIT SCORES

How are credit scores calculated? Designers of credit scoring review a set of consumers—often over a million. The credit profiles of the consumers are examined to identify common variables they exhibit. The designers then build statistical models that assign weights to each variable, and these variables are combined to create a credit score.

Models for specific types of loans, such as auto or mortgage, more closely consider consumer payment statistics related to these loans. Model builders strive to identify the best set of variables from a consumer's past credit history that most effectively predict future credit behavior. This way you can try to "predict" how their credit with your business will be. To come up with a score, information is collected from the credit report, such as bill-paying history, type of accounts listed, late payments, collection accounts, overdue accounts, and age of accounts. Credit scoring gives points for each factor to determine if a customer is likely to repay a debt.

What's in a Credit Score?

Credit scoring is a system you can use to help determine if you want to extend credit.

The information that impacts a credit score varies depending on the score being used. Credit scores are only affected by elements in a credit report, such as:

- Number of late payments
- Type, number, and age of accounts
- Total debt
- Recent inquiries
- How late payments are or were at any time

If a business card/corporate card or gas card does not appear on your credit report, it will not affect your score.

Credit scores *do not* consider:

- Your race, color, religion, national origin, sex, or marital status. U.S. law prohibits credit scoring from considering these facts, as well as any receipt of public assistance, or the exercise of any consumer right under the Consumer Credit Protection Act.
- Age

- Salary, occupation, title, employer, date employed, or employment history. However, you will consider this information in making approval decisions.
- Where the applicant lives
- Any interest rate being charged on a particular credit card or other account
- Any items reported as child/family support obligations or rental agreements
- Certain types of inquiries (requests for credit reports). The score does not count "consumer disclosure inquiry" requests made for credit reports in order to check it. It also does not count "promotional inquiries," requests made by lenders in order to make a "pre-approved" credit offer or "account review inquiry" requests made by lenders to review an account with them. Also, inquiries for employment purposes are not counted.

Things to look for if you want a good credit score:

- Bills paid on time
- Low outstanding debt
- Long credit history
- Not many recent credit inquiries
- Not many credit card accounts

Types of Credit Scores

There are primarily two types of scores—generic and custom. Custom scores are generated by individual lenders, who rely on credit reports and other information, such as account history, from their own portfolios. Generic scores are for general use in making lending decisions and are based on credit data only. The lower the score, the greater the risk of default.

Reasons to Use Credit Scores

Before credit scores, lenders (or business owners) physically looked over each customer's credit report to determine whether to grant credit and how much. A business owner might deny credit based on a subjective judgment that a consumer already held too much debt, or had too many recent late payments. Not only was this time-consuming, but also human judgment was prone to errors and bias. Businesses were using personal opinion to make a decision about a customer that may have had little bearing on the customer's ability to repay debt. You would be doing this if you didn't pull a credit report but rather just called the references on a credit application.

Credit scores help you assess risk more fairly because they are consistent and objective. They also consider information you don't have access to without pulling a credit report.

Credit Score Factors

Score factors are the elements from a credit report that drive credit scores. For example, total debt, invoices, types of accounts, number of late payments, and age of accounts affect credit scores. Score factors indicate what elements of a credit history most affected the credit score at the time it was calculated. You will be required to provide applications with the most significant score factors when they are declined credit by you. This needs to be on the denied for credit letter you send. Derogatory things to look for on a credit report when deciding whether or not to extend credit are:

- Bankruptcy filings within the past ten years

- Open tax liens and judgments, regardless of the amount and regardless of whether it was released within the past five years.
- Accounts placed for collections
- Accounts written off to bad debt
- Repossessions
- Unpaid student loans
- Total number of UCC filings with one or more of the following pledged collateral:
  - Accounts receivable
  - Inventory
  - Contracts
  - Proceeds
  - Hereafter acquired property
  - Leases
  - Notes receivable
  - Reported collection accounts
  - Telecommunications accounts that are reported as service disconnect, write off, or skipped accounts

When you check someone's credit, you are looking for a customer that is legitimate, has some credit history, and may have been in business for a while. If a business owns rather than rents the building they do business out of, they may be more stable.

IMPORTANT COLLECTION TIPS TO REMEMBER

Do not:

- Harass, oppress, or abuse someone who owes you money
- Use threats of any kind but more specifically, threats of violence or harm against the person, property, or reputation of someone who owes you money

- Publish or display in a public place a list of customers who have not paid you or gave you a bad check
- Use the telephone or e-mail to annoy the debtor
- Advertise anyone's debt to you
- Falsely imply that you are or work for an attorney or government office
- Imply that they have committed a crime
- Misrepresent the amount owed
- Imply that an attorney is involved, if one is not
- Tell customers they will be arrested if they do not pay you

- Make your letters look like legal forms when they are not
- State that you will seize, garnish, attach, or sell their property, wages, or assets unless you legally intend to take that action
- Threaten court action unless you intend to sue
- Use a false name when signing letters or making collection calls
- Deposit a post-dated check early
- Make collect calls to someone who owes you money
- Use postcards for debt collection purposes

CHAPTER 7

Creating a Credit Policy

WHEN A NEW CUSTOMER CALLS OR comes in to set up an account, you should set up the account on a pre-paid or COD basis. The customer should be sent or given a credit application if they wish to become a charge customer. Once the completed application is received, you need to run the credit check and make a decision on a credit limit. If the customer is approved you must send them a letter letting them know they have been approved and what their credit limit is. If they are denied credit, you must send them a letter letting them know they were denied and what the reasons are. There needs to be a notation on the bottom of the letter telling them where they can call or write to obtain a free copy of their credit report if they disagree with any of the information. The Credit Bureau will provide you with a sample letter to have printed with your company information on it. You need to make two copies of the letter, with the original being mailed to the customer and the copy attached to the credit application.

Following is a list of steps to maintain a credit policy:

- Have every new customer fill out a credit application and/or new account form
- Check customer's credit
- Deny or approve credit
- Send out denial or approval letter
- Lock all credit forms and information in a file cabinet
- Input credit limits into your computer on customer's accounts

IS A CREDIT MANAGER RIGHT FOR YOUR SMALL BUSINESS?

Should you hire a credit manager or can you do this yourself? You can certainly do the duties of a credit manager yourself, but you need to be educated in the procedures, policies, and laws involved. If you hire someone or outsource someone to do this for you, they should already be familiar with these aspects of the job. If you are a small business with limited funds, you might want to set up your policy yourself, and hire someone part-time.

Potential candidates for this job should be able to talk on the phone and type notes into your computer system at the same time; every contact with a debtor needs to be documented with the day, date, time, and all details of the interaction. Try talking to a candidate for the job on the phone prior to the interview. Since most of a credit manager's job is on the phone making collection calls, you want to know how they sound and if they sound confident, speak clearly, and how they handle the call generally. Being a debt collector is a very demanding job, so be sure to train and have a trial period before hiring anyone.

Use the following sample job description to evaluate resumes, drive discussions at interviews, assess candidates, and train new hires. You should customize this description to fit your agency.

Debt Collector or Credit Manager Job Description

Job Title: Debt Collector or Credit Manager

Description:
- Maintain, track, and collect on 250 accounts
- Provide quarterly reports
- Ensure compliance with all state and federal laws
- Read, interpret, and apply laws, rules, regulations, policies, and procedures

- Make decisions or solve problems by using logic, identifying key facts, exploring alternatives, and proposing high-quality solutions

Required Skills:
- Computer experience
- Credit management knowledge
- Skip-tracing knowledge
- Mediation
- Negotiation
- Communication
- Patience
- Good follow-up skills
- Required skills: Collect debtor accounts by phone and mail
- Attend credit meetings and seminars
- Perform some field collections
- Know the FDCPA and FCRA
- Appear in court occasionally
- Research disputes
- Provide documentation to support debts
- Other tasks as needed or as assigned

Other Requirements: This job will be done while sitting, but there may be some walking, standing, bending, carrying of light items such as papers or books, or driving an automobile. No special physical demands are required to perform the work.

You and your collectors should be able to:
- Identify the most common forms of credit activity
- Name the three major credit reporting agencies and their function in credit extension
- List five important federal laws and their roles in governing the credit lifecycle
- Describe why listening is important and name three components of active listening
- Identify the differences between assertive and aggressive communication
- Know how to open and close a collection call with courtesy

- Know how to ask fact-finding questions based on the reason for delinquency
- Know strategies for motivating debtors at different stages of delinquency

Also, a bill collector and a small business owner must:
- Be interested in people, and be a good communicator both verbally and in writing
- Be persuasive and persistent, with the sensitivity to deal fairly with people in often difficult situations
- Be able to stay calm under pressure, and be adaptable in sometimes tricky situations
- Have strong negotiation skills and the ability to explain financial matters firmly and clearly
- Have mathematical ability to explain payments, financial terms, and credit services and policies
- Be able to understand relevant legislation concerning data protection and harassment
- Have office administration and computer skills

SKILLS AND RESOURCES FOR CREDIT MANAGERS OR ANY SMALL BUSINESS OWNER

The following tools are essential for a credit manager to effectively do their job. Without even one of these tools, there will be a crack through which a debtor may slip.

- Signed credit application
- Full knowledge of The Fair Debt Collection Practices Act and additional laws particular to the state in which you are collecting.
- Communication skills
- Negotiation skills
- Skip-tracing or locating skills
- Mediation skills
- Organization skills

Following is an outline of some areas you may

want to get training in.

Developing a Telephone Voice

When you make collection calls, you need to have your "debt collector" voice. You need to sound confident, in control, and upbeat. Don't even make the call if you are unsure of what to say, feel flustered, or are not confident. Try listening to your voice; you can call yourself and leave a message on your voice mail or answering machine. When you listen to the message, remember this is what a customer or debtor will hear when you call. Things to listen for when you replay your message are:

- Do you sound pleasant?
- Do you sound confident?
- Do you sound intelligent?
- Is your speech clear?
- Do you come across as professional?
- Do you speak too fast?
- Do you sound tired?
- Are you mumbling?
- Is your voice too loud or too soft?
- Does your message seem drab or boring?
- Do you say "um"?

When you listen to your voice, take notes on what you don't like about your message and try to work on those things. Try working on one thing a day or a week. You will get comfortable with the change and it will become natural. You also can ask a friend, family member, or colleague to listen to your message and tell you their honest opinion on what they thought when they heard it. Here are some tips to get you started:

1. Smile! Even though you are on the phone, your smile comes through in your speech.

2. Sit up straight.
3. Be focused; don't answer e-mails while you are making calls.

As a collector you will need to know how to handle difficult people and cope with rude callers effectively; you will want to have prepared series of correctly pronounced useful replies; you will need to be able to use common sense, responsibility, and integrity. You also will want to improve your nonvisual impression. When you are a collector your impression with the debtor is left through your voice. You want to speak clearly and have control, no wavering or saying "um." You also could try voice exercises to project a stronger, friendlier personality. There will be times that you will also have to control your anger—something the debtor or customer says may suddenly anger you or be insulting to you and you need to stop, breathe deep, and respond professionally.

Refining Listening Skills

When you call a debtor and you state the reason for your call or ask a question, wait for them to answer. No matter how long the pause is, let them break the silence. When you ask your questions and the customer or debtor begins to answer you, stay silent and listen. Do not multitask, focus on the customer's account screen or invoice, or look at an object on your desk; just listen. When you are listening, pay attention because you can listen and hear just enough to get the "idea" of what someone is saying or you can focus on really listening and also understand what is being said and then make an appropriate response quickly, which keeps you in control of the call and the situation.

Following is a listing of some useful skills needed to be a good listener:

- Being able to pay full attention
- Being able to focus
- Waiting for a speaker to completely finish speaking and not interrupting

When you make a collection call you want to make the customer or debtor feel understood. You can empathize with them but you need to be firm and have a conclusion to your call.

Managing the Emotional Side

Debtors will get upset that you are calling them. They will cry, yell, swear, and hang up on you. When a debtor starts telling you his life story or despair and how this affects why he cannot pay, you need to be able to have compassion for the situation but offer a solution to get the debt paid. You can suggest a payment plan or different options for payment. You also need to be prepared to avoid emotional involvement—this is very difficult at times.

Preparing the Pre-Call Plan

Before you ever make a collection call you need to research the account. Before you dial you need to know the invoice number, date, amount that is past due, how past due it is, the payment history, details of the order, and if there were any disputed items. When the debtor asks you a question you need to answer immediately whenever possible. This shows the debtor that you are serious, you know what you are doing, and you have all your ducks in a row.

Making Your Opening Statement

Your opening statement should be brief and to the point. You need to identify yourself and your company, state why you are calling, and what you want. An example would be: "Hi, this is Michelle from KTM Auto calling about your balance of $500.00 on invoice #1234 dated 4/1/06. I am calling today to take your payment over the phone to clear this balance from your account. Would you like to pay with a check over the phone, debit, or credit card?" **Stop!** Let the debtor break the silence after your question and remember, always assume the debtor will pay.

Ask questions with precision and make the transition to the payment arrangement. All your questions should be clear and to the point with silence after each question. Following is a sample phone conversation.

Debtor: I can't pay, I don't have any money.
Collector: Are you working?
Debtor: Yes, but I just started a job and don't get paid for two weeks.
Collector: What day will you get paid?
Debtor: Friday.
Collector: Okay, then you can mail a money order (or check) for $25 on Saturday.

This example can go so many different ways depending on the debtor's responses. You have to be positive and get them to agree to make a payment. Once you reiterate what is going to happen, send them a confirmation letter with a payment envelope. Then call them on Friday to remind them about mailing the payment. An example of what you could say would be, "Hi, this is Michelle from KTM Auto, calling to confirm that you will be mailing a money order for $25 tomorrow, Saturday morning."

You need to become familiar with common debtor objections. The best way to do this is to make collection calls yourself. Some common objections and responses follow:

Objection: I can't make a payment over the phone. I don't have a credit card or checking account.
Reponse: You can Western Union the money to me, or mail a money order.

Objection: I don't have any money.
Response: How do you pay your utilities? Set up smaller payments for awhile or ask them to borrow from a family member.\

Objection: I lost the invoice.
Response: Fax the invoice if possible, and call right back or mail the invoice and follow up with a call.

Objection: I didn't' receive the item.
Response: Get proof of delivery from the shipper.

Closing the Call

Your last statement should reiterate everything covered in the call. Repeat all actions that will be taken. For example: "Okay, on Saturday you will mail a money order for $25 in the envelope I send you today. Then you will send $25 a month every Saturday until May 15th."

Some useful resources for you:

The Fair Debt Collection Practices Act: www.credit-and-collections.com/resources-fairdebt.html

State laws listed by state: www.lawdog.com/state/laws.htm

Information on communication skills: www.inc.com/guides/growth/23032.html

Information on negotiating: www.salestrainingamerica.com/negotians_training.htm

Information on mediation: www.mediate.com

A site with helpful tools for organization: www.shopget-organized.com

Printed products such as small or large payment envelopes and more: www.challengebp.com search.asp?keyword-Pay%20Envelope

You can also have these printed at any printer's office or supply store. Or, you can purchase boxes of small-sized envelopes and a self-inking stamp with your return address on it and create your own for less.)

Past due stickers: www.rentons.com

FOLLOWING FEDERAL AND STATE LAWS WHEN EXTENDING CREDIT

If your business does grant credit, you must comply with federal laws affecting credit sales to consumers. Also, states are beginning to adopt consumer credit laws that mirror federal law. One of the laws you should become familiar with is the Truth in Lending Act. This law requires you to disclose your exact credit terms to credit applicants and regulates how you advertise consumer credit. Among the items you must disclose to a consumer who buys on credit are monthly finance charges, annual interest rate, terms or when payment is due, the total price, and the price if any late fees are added or any other fees they may be responsible for if they don't pay on time such as court or attorney fees. This statute attempts to ensure that customers know what they're getting into.

Another law to familiarize yourself with is the Fair Credit Billing Act; this law explains what to do if a customer claims you made a mistake in your billing. The customer must notify you within 60 days after you mailed the first bill containing the claimed error. You must respond within 30 days unless the dispute has already been resolved. You also must conduct a reasonable investigation and, within 90 days of getting the customer's letter, explain why your bill is correct or else correct the error.

If you don't follow this procedure, you must give the customer a $50 credit toward the disputed amount—even if your bill was correct. Until the dispute is resolved, you can't report to a credit bureau that the customer is delinquent. In addition to telling you how to handle billing disputes, the Fair Credit Billing Act requires you, in periodic mailings, to tell consumers what their rights are.

The Fair Credit Billing Act only covers "open end" credit accounts, such as revolving charge accounts, like credit card accounts. It does not cover installment contracts, loans, or extensions of credit you repay on a fixed schedule. Consumers often buy cars, furniture, and major appliances on an installment basis, and repay personal loans in installments as well; these types of "extensions of credit" are not covered by this law.

The Equal Credit Opportunity Act is a law that prohibits discrimination against a credit applicant on the basis of race, color, religion, national origin, age, sex, or marital status. This Act does leave you free to consider legitimate factors in granting credit, such as the applicant's financial status (earnings and savings) and credit record. Despite the prohibition on age discrimination, you can deny a consumer who hasn't reached the legal age for entering into contracts.

The Fair Credit Reporting Act is intended to protect consumers from having their eligibility for credit marred by incomplete or misleading credit report information. The law gives consumers the right to a copy of their credit report. If they see an inaccurate item, they can ask that it be corrected or removed. If the business reporting the credit problem doesn't agree to a change or deletion or if the credit bureau refuses to make it, the consumer can add a 100-word statement to the file explaining his or her side of the story. This becomes a part of any future credit report.

COMPLYING WITH THE FAIR DEBT COLLECTION PRACTICES ACT

The Fair Debt Collection Practices Act (FDCPA) is geared mostly toward third-party collectors. Small business owners are more directly affected by state laws that apply directly to collection methods used by a creditor or business owner. It is my recommendation that you make yourself familiar with these laws, as you create and implement your credit policy. It is a good idea to know what the laws are and follow them as closely as possible, even if they are not required by your state or the state you are collecting in.

Small business owners who grant credit should know the FDCPA because:

- Credit grantors' collection practices are covered by the law under certain conditions.
- Credit grantors should know what their collection services and attorney may and may not do under the law, especially if they hire them to do collection, as it is a reflection on them and their business.
- Creditors may be liable with respect to the collection practices of third-party debt collectors under Section 5 of the Federal Trade Commission Act and in some cases under their state laws.

- Credit grantors must comply with FDCPA when they collect their own debts using a name other than their own. For example, if Dunn's Oil Company uses the name The Dunn Collection Service to collect its own debts, they must comply. If several hospitals or doctors' offices join in a "shared hospital/medical services" concept and collect their own debts through a collection service with a name other than that of the hospital or doctors' office, they must comply.
- If a credit grantor mails a series of collection letters that carry a business name other than the company's and that are not clearly showing that they are affiliated with the creditor, then the credit grantor must comply.
- Also, some financial institutions, such as banks and credit unions, become debt collectors when they ask for help from another bank when a debtor has relocated, so then the bank must comply.
- If you add interest, late fees, or delinquency charges on accounts, your collection agency or credit manager needs to be aware of this. Under FDCPA, your collectors are allowed to add interest and other charges to the past due amount if the agreement or contract creating the debt allows it or if it is permitted by state law.
- The law permits you to contact a third party in order to locate a debtor you cannot find, if the mail is returned, or the phone is disconnected. If you have good information on the original credit application, you may contact anyone on the credit application to obtain information on the debtor without disclosing why you are looking for them. When you

contact anyone, you cannot reveal that you are calling about a past due balance.

- If you receive a payment on an account you have placed with an outside collection agency, you should immediately notify the collection service. An agency that continues to try to collect on a debt that has been paid could be charged with harassment or use of false representation. You, as a credit grantor, could be held jointly responsible.

PENALTIES FOR VIOLATING THE FDCPA

Credit managers or business owners who are attempting to collect debts owed can be fined up to $1,000 plus actual damages for violating the FDCPA. A collector who acted in good faith and made a bona fide error is not liable for such penalties.

Some practices that are prohibited by law are:

- You may not charge debtors for collect telephone calls or telegrams made.
- You may not solicit a postdated check for the purpose of threatening criminal prosecution.
- You may add certain charges to the account if state law permits or the agreement or contract creating the debt so allows.
- You may accept postdated checks. If a check is postdated by more than 5 days, you must send the debtor a written notice of intent to deposit that check not more than 10 or less than 3 business days prior to depositing the check.

ELEMENTS OF A CREDIT POLICY

There are six elements to a credit policy:

1. Completing the new account form
2. Completing the credit application
3. Checking credit
4. Setting credit limits
5. Notifying the customer
6. Updating credit limits

New Account Forms

The new account form is not required, but can be helpful to you. This can be a form of general information, such as name, address, contact information, how you heard about us, who do you currently use for this service and what has been your experience with that company, and why do you want to change companies. This will help you to provide better customer service to your customers. If you know what they want and what they didn't like about another company, you can become outstanding to them. This also will tell you which of your advertising methods are working; if they saw your ad in the paper, or heard about you on the radio, or maybe by word of mouth. You should always ask who referred them and send that customer a thank you and maybe offer them a discount on their next purchase.

Credit Applications

If you don't implement a credit policy or do anything else mentioned in this book, the one thing you should do to protect yourself and your business is to always get a credit application. If I had to tell you one thing to do to help your credit policy, if you decided not to do anything else, it would be to get a credit application. This will help you in so many ways if you do not get paid.

Be sure to include something such as "The undersigned authorizes inquiry as to credit information. I/We acknowledge that credit privileges, if granted, may be withdrawn at any time." When you receive a completed credit application from someone, check it to be sure it is signed, filled out completely, and readable. Make sure to give the customer a copy and keep the original for your records.

Checking Credit

When you check credit you can do it a few different ways. You can become a member of one of the credit bureaus and pull credit reports for review; you can use an online service or manually call the personal, business, and bank references listed on the credit application. All of these will work. A credit report is the best way to go, but if you are a new business and can't afford to become a member right away, manually calling references takes some time but is worth it in the long run.\

Setting Credit Limits

Setting credit limits without a credit report is a little tougher. You have to decide what this person makes for a salary and what their expenses might be. Without a credit report you don't know if the customer has any credit cards, if they are past due. or even if they have been placed for collection before. If you call and check references and get a very good bank reference, you might want to start with a credit limit that allows the customer to make purchases on credit but maybe pay any outstanding balance before more credit is extended. Each situation will need your judgment.

Notifying the Customer

When you run a credit report on someone you need to notify them in writing if they were approved or denied credit. I have included a sample of each type of letter for you in this book.

Updating Credit Limits

You might want to re-check credit once or twice a year on customers, or maybe if you read something in a trade journal about a company having financial issues, you might want to check their credit and re-evaluate the credit limit they have with you. If you change the credit limit, whether to increase or decrease, you must notify the customer and give them the reasons why.

PART III

Managing Business Finances

CHAPTER 8

Handling Customer Deductions

YOU HAVE A CREDIT-APPROVED CUStomer that has been doing business with you for a couple of months now. They have been paying on time and making steady orders. Suddenly you receive a check with a deduction on it. It might just be a negative number on the check stub, or maybe the check is just for less with no explanation. Deductions can impair your cash flow and take up valuable time, so you want to take care of them right away. The more time that goes by once you receive a deduction, the harder it will be to get it paid if it is not legitimate.

When you receive a payment with a deduction, research the deduction immediately. If you need to provide paperwork to the customer regarding the deduction, call them and tell them it is coming and ask if they need any other specific documentation that you can include. Mail the paperwork and use certified mail with a signature, or a flat rate priority mail envelope. When you receive notification that they have the documents, call them right away to find out the status. Do not get caught up in the game of sending the documentation two or three times—this is a stalling tactic. Stay on top of the situation and resolve it as quickly as possible. You also could fax or e-mail the documentation for quicker resolution. Make sure the customer sends the payment immediately upon resolution; do not allow another 30 days or any more time to pass.

DETERMINING THE CAUSE OF DEDUCTIONS

If you receive a check for less than the amount owed with no explanation, you need to find out the reason for this. The easiest and quickest way is to pick up the phone and call your customer. Explain that you have received check #123 and it is

$50 short. They will probably put you on hold to go check it out and can hopefully come back to the phone with an immediate answer. Maybe there was a shortage on a delivery, or they felt they should get a discount; it can be so many different things. Once you know what the deduction is for, it will be easy for you to clear it up and decide if it is a deduction you want to accept or deny. Do not wait. It is imperative that you resolve the deduction immediately. I have worked as a credit manager at so many companies that would have all these random balances on the books from customers that took deductions on a check. The company would either not research or not follow through on the deduction and it would never get paid. Once too much time goes by it is harder to clear up any deductions. The situation is no longer clear in everyone's mind, the checks have been filed and need to be found and looked up—you may need to request a proof of delivery and the longer you wait, the harder that may be to obtain.

HEADING OFF FUTURE DEDUCTIONS

If you have a customer who takes frequent deductions, you will want to note this on their account and maybe re-evaluate your credit terms with them. You can incorporate something into your credit policy in regard to deductions and make sure your customers are aware of this policy. You can ask that all deductions be pre-approved or be required to have accompanying documentation to support them when they are deducted from a payment. This way if these things don't happen, or you have a customer over 120 days past due who sends a check for less,

claiming some deductions, you have something to fall back on. Some customers who are having financial problems will take deductions on very old invoices as a way to pay less or not appear to be so delinquent.

DOCUMENTING DISCUSSIONS WITH CUSTOMERS

No matter what software you use to handle your accounts receivables you want a Notes section on every customer's account. Every transaction, piece of correspondence, order, payment, and statement should be documented. Try to include the day, date, time, and whom you spoke with in your notes. This is very important and will help you if you have a discrepancy with deductions, payments, or orders. This will also help you if the account ever gets past due and has to be taken to court or placed with an outside collection agency.

FOLLOW UP ON ERRONEOUS DEDUCTIONS

What do you do if your customer deducted money from their monthly payment and you called to be told it was a mistake and they will repay it on the next bill or maybe they are sending a separate check for the deduction, and it does not arrive? You want to follow up immediately, offer to go over and pick up the check, and try to get them to pay over the phone with a check or credit card. It is up to you to express urgency of this matter so they will take it seriously. If the repayment is not forthcoming you might want to let them know you cannot process any more orders until this is paid. The longer you leave this open on your books, the harder it will be to collect. If more than one month goes by, when you call again about the deduction, you may be starting over at step one. They may have to research the deduction again, or put you off telling you that it has to be approved by someone else and that person is not available, or many other excuses I have heard over the years. Once you make the initial call on the deduction and are told it will be re-paid, you should send a certified letter with a payment envelope reiterating the facts of the conversation.

For example, you could write:

Dear (whoever you spoke to):

As per our conversation today (day and date) I am enclosing an addressed payment envelope for your re-payment of a $50 deduction taken in error on your check # 123. You can then call if you don't receive the payment, and speak to whoever you addressed the letter to or the person who signed for the certified letter, if it is a different person. Even though the deduction was taken in error, it is left up to you to get your payment—the same as when a full invoice is past due.

HOW SMALL BUSINESS OWNERS CAN HANDLE DELINQUENT ACCOUNTS

Once you have a credit policy in place your delinquent accounts should not get out of control. It is up to you or your credit manager to monitor them so your customers follow the policy and don't get out of control. Even if you have the greatest credit policy in the world, when you extend credit, you put your business at risk. You need to monitor your accounts receivable aging reports and send out dunning notices and make

collection calls to any accounts that start to get past due. It is up to you to keep control of the balances outstanding that affect your cash flow.

Categorize your accounts by past due amount owed and how many days late. Then put them into groups by how you think they will pay. For example, if you decide there is a very good possibility certain customers *will* pay, put those accounts together and start collection action on those first. Then work on the accounts you think *might* pay followed by the small-balance accounts, over six-month-old accounts, or accounts where the mail is returned.

LETTERS TO SEND TO DELINQUENT ACCOUNTS

1. Friendly Reminder
2. Second Notice
3. Final Notice

When you create your credit forms and collection letters or notices, you need to remember that there are certain state and federal requirements you must follow. Some tips for making your forms and letters "work":

- Speak or write in simple terms, rather than using big words and legal jargon, if you can avoid it.
- Don't ramble on or repeat yourself.
- Make sure after reading the notice or form, the customer knows everything you want them to know about your credit policy.
- Did you include everything you needed to include to be compliant with all laws?
- Is your language clear?
- Is the type easy to read?

- Is it organized?
- Does your letter have "white space" or is it crowded?
- Be blunt and to the point while maintaining professionalism.

Be sure to review any credit or collection forms with your attorney to be sure you are in compliance with any laws including those under the Uniform Consumer Credit Code (U.C.C.C.). Be sure your applications, forms, and letters relate to your customers. Depending on the education level, average age, or income of your customers you may need to adjust your forms and letters so that they are easily understood. Words you may want to avoid in your contract, forms, and letters might be:

- Heretofore
- Hereinafter
- Hereinabove
- Herein
- Foregoing
- Aforesaid
- Aforementioned
- Thereof
- Hereby
- Assent

I have included some sample letters for you here that you can modify to suit your business or use as they are. This is a series of three letters you can use when an account first becomes past due. The first one is a friendly reminder—you would send this when the account is up to 10 days past due. If you don't receive payment then, you would send the second notice 7 to 10 days after that. I would make a phone call in between the first two letters as well. If you still do not receive

payment I would put the account on hold and send the final notice. Remember to change your collection letters frequently—you can make them stronger and more action-oriented.

Friendly Reminder Letter

Date

Dear

Please be advised that your account has a past due balance of $100 that was due on Date. Please send your payment of $100 today in the enclosed payment envelope to bring your account current.

Please call this office at (000)000-0000 if there is a reason you have not paid this balance. Thank you for your prompt attention to this important matter.

Sincerely,

Second Notice

Date

Dear

We sent you a first notice on Date, requesting your payment of $100 to clear up the past due balance on your account. To date, we have not had a response or received your payment.

Your payment, or any questions you may have, should be directed to this office to ensure proper credit to your account. You may also pay online at www.michelledunn.com for your payment to be immediately credited to your account.

Sincerely,

Final Notice

> Date
>
> Dear
>
> Because you have failed to respond to our previous letters, this is an attempt at an amicable resolution of your account.
>
> Unless your remittance reaches our office within the next seven (7) days, we will be forced to take further action. We urge you to send your payment today or call to pay by credit card or with a check by phone. You can also pay online at **www.michelledunn.com.**
>
> TOLL FREE 1-800-300-1234
>
> Your Business Mailing Address
>
> We would like to resolve this matter and put it behind us as much as you would.
>
> But we are committed to taking whatever steps are necessary and proper to enforce payment of your obligation.
>
> Sincerely,

To show urgency with any of these letters you can send them by certified mail with return receipt requested or you can send them in a Priority Mail flat rate envelope, which is cheaper and will still get opened right away. If you use online postage you can get delivery confirmation for free using Click-N-Ship at www.usps.com.

Your first letter lets your customer know you are on top of your accounts and don't really appreciate having to spend time and money sending them a letter to advise them of this fact. Your second letter lets them know that you have not forgotten them and you are not backing down. You take your money seriously and don't work for free. Your third letter is the last straw. Now they know you're extremely unhappy with them. They know they need to make good or not show their face in your office or store again. They know they will not be able to do business with you again and that you will probably give them a poor credit reference if ever asked.

MAKING QUALITY COLLECTION CALLS

Before you ever make a collection call, you need to look in the computer or customer folder to see what has been done on the account. Any time you speak to a customer you need to make a note in the comments screen of their account or a handwritten note in their file. You should always put the date first followed by what was said. Then if you call a customer or they call you, you have the information instantly. This is extremely helpful if more than one person is dealing with the customers. If you leave a message and the customer calls back, anyone who answers the phone will see who spoke to them last, on what day and time, and what was said.

The first collection call should be made when an account is 45 days old if your terms are net 30. You would have already sent out a friendly reminder, so if they have not sent payment yet, your call should not be a surprise. This will be a friendly call to remind them about the bill and make sure they have a copy of the invoice. You also will ask them when the check was mailed and what the check number, amount, and date were.

The second call would be made if payment is not received within a week of the first call. This call will refer back to the first call, where they said there wasn't a problem and they were sending out the payment.

The third and any follow-up calls will be made if payment is not received within a week of the last call. These calls would be made weekly until there is a satisfactory payment schedule.

Your collection call should start with you identifying yourself, then stating why you are calling, asking for the payment, and waiting for an answer. You want the call to motivate the customer to pay you so you need to know how to communicate in a friendly, persuasive manner.

What You Can and Cannot Do

Once you place the collection call to the customer, you must only speak to the owner of the business or an authorized bookkeeper if the account is a business. If the account is a consumer debt, only speak to the person who owes the money or their spouse. *Never* discuss past due accounts with an unauthorized person, such as a receptionist, neighbor, friend, or relative, other than a spouse.

Purpose of the Collection Call

The purpose of a collection call is for you to get paid. You need to communicate in a way that encourages your customer to pay you and be happy about it. You want to do this as quickly and efficiently as possible while getting the desired result. When you make collection calls, stay in charge of the call or you could be sitting on the phone for 20 minutes listening to someone explain to you about their sick children, broken down car, and lack of a job, and all the other reasons they just can't send you any money.

Once you have the customer on the phone, identify yourself and your company, and state the purpose of your call. If the customer tells you they cannot pay anything, listen to their story and then explain that you understand that they cannot pay the whole balance at this time, but that you do need a payment. Start at 80 percent of what is due and go down from there.

The purpose of your call is to get a payment, no matter how big or small—ideally it will be in full but sometimes that is not realistic. Remember, this is the time to set up payment arrangements if they cannot pay in full. Also remember, if you set the customer up on a payment plan, you might want to re-evaluate their credit terms. You don't want to continue extending credit to a customer who is making payments on a balance that they cannot pay off in full.

At the end of the call, repeat the payment schedule to the debtor and make a note in the comments screen. Whenever you make a payment arrangement like this, you need to send a follow-up letter the same day with the same information in the letter as was stated on the phone. A good idea is to include a payment envelope with the letter. The easier you make it for the debtor to make a payment, the better your chances of being paid. You may even want to provide a postage-paid envelope or at least an envelope pre-printed with your company address.

FOLLOW UP

The letters you send need to be kept in a tickler file with a follow-up date written on them, usually a week later. Then on that day you need to pull the letters and check to see if payments have been received. If not, you need to call them immediately. If they make a partial payment, send them a letter thanking them for that payment and telling them their new balance and when you expect the next payment. Be very clear and to the point. Put a copy of this letter in your tickler file with a date of a week later to follow up.

COLLECTION CALLS, TIPS, AND EXAMPLES

Making collection calls is somewhat of an art. Once you do it long enough you can almost anticipate what the debtor is about to say. You need to be on top of your accounts and then on top of the call. You need to know what to say to every response while maintaining professionalism and staying within the law.

Some advantages of collection calls include:

- They are inexpensive, compared to personal visits and individually typed letters.
- They are immediate in that they produce some sort of answer the moment the contact is made.
- They are personal, allowing an exchange between two people.
- They are informative, allowing you to ask questions, obtain information, and take appropriate action.
- They are flexible in that your approach can be varied as changing situations demand.

Following are some tips for effective collection calls:

- The call should result in agreement as to what is to be done.
- Use voice mail or answering machines if available. Leave detailed complete messages and speak slowly.
- Always be courteous.
- When asked why you are calling, never say it is in regard to a debt; regarding an invoice is better.
- Create a sense of urgency by leaving a deadline time in which to hear back from them.
- Get the name of the person in charge of issuing checks and paying bills.
- Ask for the best time to call them in the future.
- Leave complete messages, your name, company name, phone number, and the request for a return call.
- Get the name of the person taking the message.
- Ask when the person you need to speak with will be back, and call at that time.
- When speaking to a debtor use their name and/or appropriate titles, such as Dr., Mrs., or Mr.

Here is an example of how a debt collection call could go and some possible responses:

Collector: Mr. Smith, this is Bob from Acme Tools. We have not received your monthly payment of $100 toward your account.

Mr. Smith: You didn't send me an envelope.

Collector: Whether we send you an envelope or not you must make your monthly payments to avoid further action on your account. I can take your payment now over the phone and give you the mailing address for the next payment. I will also send you a confirmation letter with your new balance after today's payment is posted, and will include a payment envelope.

No matter how ridiculous this might sound to you, this response is given a lot more than you think. The collector took care of every aspect of the situation and left the debtor no way out of the phone call or the payment. Notice how he stayed in control of the call and offered reasonable solutions to the current problem and to avoid a future problem. Next month if the collector has to call, the debtor would look like a fool to say, "I didn't receive an envelope."

Here is another example:

Mr. Smith: I never received a bill.

Collector: What is your address?

This way you can verify the address you have on file and where bills are sent. You should verify this with the customer, as well as all other contact information including a fax number. Then you can hang up or fax the invoice while you are on the phone and verify they received it and find out when the check will be sent.

Another possible scenario is:

Mr. Smith: We sent a check.

Collector: Great! What day did you send the check? Can you please tell me the check number and amount? Can I have the address you mailed it to?

This forces the customer to look up the information if it was in fact mailed and if it was not it prompts the customer to send a check since he is now giving you a check number. Also, he will lose face if he gives you all this information and you

have to call back in a couple of days to find out where the check is. You must be ready to ask questions about whatever answer they throw at you. You must be ready to provide a reasonable solution so they do not have a way out of paying or stalling payment. If you don't have an answer ready, you lose control of the call and they will just give you another excuse.

CONFIRMATION LETTERS

When you make a collection call, especially if you leave a message, you want to send a confirmation letter. If a customer knows they are past due and comes back from lunch to a message from you, and does not return the call, then a couple of days later receives a letter and another call, your bill will be moved to the top of the pile.

I am including a sample letter for a confirmation of a payment promise and a confirmation of a payment plan. Any time you set up a payment plan or someone tells you they are sending you a check, send these letters.

Confirmation of a Payment Promise Letter

Date

Dear

This letter is to confirm the commitment you made in our telephone conversation. You stated that a check would be mailed on DATE in the amount of $100.00.

Thank you in advance for your payment.

Sincerely,

Confirmation of a Payment Plan Letter

Date

Dear

This letter is to confirm the commitment you made on the phone today. As agreed, you will send $25 a week starting Friday, November 4, 2007 by postal mail in the form of a check to YOUR BUSINESS ADDRESS. You will then send $25 every Friday until the balance is paid in full. Until this balance is paid, all new orders will be on a pre-paid basis.

Enclosed please find a payment envelope for your first payment.

Sincerely,

TIPS FOR COLLECTING MONEY

- Don't feel guilty asking for the money, unless you like working for free.
- Develop a credit policy or "payment rules."
- Keep on top of late payers.
- Hire a credit manager or outsource your accounts receivables if you cannot do it yourself.
- Contact customers immediately if they become past due.
- Set up payment plans on the full amount due.
- Be firm and don't accept excuses.
- Be professional.

DEBT COLLECTION "CHEAT SHEET"

- Debtors cannot be put in jail because of failure to pay a debt.
- You can sue a debtor if they start making small monthly payments and you did not agree to accept them.
- *Always* record the date, time of day, name, and contact information of the person you call.
- Recording phone conversations without the consent of the other party is legal in some states.
- You cannot visit a debtor's home or call them before 8 a.m. or after 8:30 p.m.
- You cannot call a debtor at work if you know the employer does not allow this.
- You can contact other people to find debtors, but you cannot tell them it is because they owe money.
- If a debtor gives you an attorney's name, you can only contact the attorney.
- A debtor can stop you from calling by telling you not to call anymore.
- You cannot use threats of violence, profanity, or any false statements.
- Repeated use of a telephone to annoy or harass or give false credit information about a debtor to anyone is prohibited.

PART IV

When to Use a Collection Agency

You should use a collection agency when you have past due accounts on your books that you are not receiving regular payments on, the customer is ignoring you and your phone calls and letters, or their phone is disconnected or their mail is returned as undeliverable or moved, left no forwarding address, or if you are getting many excuses. If the debtor has the ability to pay, a collection agency can help you get your money. You might use an agency when you just don't have the time to both chase your money and run your business. Many agencies offer an outsourcing option on accounts receivables that you can use before placing the account "for collection." Collection agencies specialize in this type of work–they do it all day, every day, and are able to provide quality results.

CHAPTER 9

How to Choose a Collection Agency for Your Small Business

Choosing a professional collection service to manage delinquent accounts and other related tasks is a wise decision. The agency should represent your organization in a responsible and professional manner, and provide a satisfactory rate of recovery while maintaining your public image. This decision involves more than just giving your business to the lowest bidder—it requires careful consideration.

Consider the following qualifications and credentials when choosing a collection service.

- Is the agency a member of a national trade association? Membership is an indication of professional integrity.
- Does the agency belong to a local Chamber of Commerce or Rotary Club?

- Does the agency charge fees that are clearly stated?
- Does the agency specialize in a certain type of collections?
- Is the agency prepared to give the best possible service? An agency cannot guarantee results on any specific date, but will often estimate on average recovery rate that one can expect.
- Will the agency be sensitive to a consumer's individual situation? The agency should promptly notify you when it discovers a consumer who is a hardship case and recommend a proper procedure to follow.
- Make sure the agency complies with all state laws and the FDCPA.
- Check to see if the agency holds memberships in state or national trade associations or is a member of the Better Business Bureau.

- How many collectors does the agency have? How many years experience do they have?

The relationship you have with your agency should be a partnership—they will help you collect your money.

WHEN TO USE A COLLECTION AGENCY

As an account ages, the chances of collecting on it decrease dramatically. It's expensive to carry accounts that you will not be able to collect using the methods at your disposal. It sometimes becomes a better use of your company's time and resources to concentrate on other aspects of your business. You might do this by hiring a credit manager, to do the collection work you have been doing, but as your business grows, you may then have to place the accounts with an outside collection agency. Using a collection agency can be profitable for your business and help you grow. Some collection agencies charge more for older accounts; this is because they are much harder to collect.

A professional collection service can assist you in collecting accounts that remain delinquent. Collectors have a vast knowledge of collection techniques, technology, and compliance issues. Using a professional collection service will save time and likely yield better results than you can achieve on your own.

When accounts reach 90 to 120 days past due, you may want to consider placing them with a collection agency. Some people place accounts at 60 days; some wait over a year—it is completely up to you. If you wait over a year it is unlikely you will get paid, but possible. If you are letting something sit on your books and grow older without

actively pursuing it, it is worth it to give it to a collection agency. It is not going to get collected if you keep it, and the percentage you will pay the agency will be well worth it.

Look for the following signs that indicate that you may need to work with a collection agency:

- A new customer does not respond to the first letter. For some unknown reason, the consumer will not or cannot pay. Potential losses could be kept to a minimum by prompt referral to a collection agency.
- Payment terms fail. In some cases irresponsible consumers pay when and if they want to. This group is responsible for 25 to 50 percent of the cost of collections. Cost and potential losses are reduced by quick action.
- The consumer makes repetitious, unfounded complaints. Such consumers are often better handled by a collection agency. You have to decide if this is worth your time or would you rather pay an agency a small percentage for that time and still get paid.
- The consumer totally denies responsibility. Without professional help, these accounts are usually written off as total losses. This is when it is good to have a signed credit application or contract and also, if possible, proof of the order and who placed it.
- Delinquency coexists with serious marital difficulties. These also require professional collection help, with the added urgency of obtaining payments before the disappearance of one or both of the responsible parties. If divorced people say the other is responsible, get a copy of the divorce decree, which will state who is responsible.

- Repeated delinquencies occur along with frequent changes of address or jobs. This group is responsible for 90 percent of all "skips." A skip is a consumer who has moved without informing creditors or leaving a forwarding address. The chance of finding a consumer and collecting a debt will decrease over time, so quick action is important. Most agencies provide a skip-tracing service.
- Obvious financial irresponsibility is apparent. In such cases, little hope exists for voluntary payments and a quick settlement.
- There is an unauthorized transfer or disposal of goods delivered in a conditional sales contract.

WORKING WITH A COLLECTION AGENCY

Once you decide on a collection agency, use their forms to list accounts or their format to upload accounts electronically. Give as much information as possible—accurate information about the account will improve collections.

In all cases, the minimum information should include:

- The correct name, address, and telephone number of the debtor
- Name of the debtor's spouse, if applicable
- Whether mail has been returned
- Debtor's and/or spouse's occupation or last known occupation and phone number
- Names of relatives, friends, neighbors, and references
- Summary of any disputes
- Date of last transaction, order, or payment

- Cellular phone, fax, e-mail address
- Nicknames or aliases, maiden name

If you have had all new customers fill out a credit application, all of the above information should be listed on there. The summary of disputes would be in the computer notes for the customer's account. This makes it very easy—all the information you need, basically all in one place, on one piece of paper. This is one of the reasons why a credit application is so important.

Cooperate with your collection agency. Rely on their experience, diligence, and judgment for the best and quickest results and promptly refer any contact from the debtor to the collection agency.

Make sure that your collection agency is familiar with the nature of your goods or services—some agencies even specialize in collecting on specific services. For example, you might find an agency that only collects on delinquent auto loans, or medical bills, or hot tub sales. If you find an agency that specializes in your field, check them out, there is a reason they only do those types of collections.

Do not place any accounts with more than one agency. Make sure that if you change collection agencies, the accounts are only being worked on by one agency.

Collection agencies' fees are based on results, not on time spent on the account. Don't expect payments to be made immediately.

HOW COLLECTION AGENCIES GET PAID

Most collection agencies charge a commission or percentage based on the many factors of the accounts they are trying to collect. Some agencies charge a flat monthly fee, and some charge per letter or call.

If an agency charges a commission, it will normally be a percentage for "standard" accounts. That would be accounts that are maybe 60 days old, have a good address and phone number, and the debt is probably collectible. My collection rate was 25 percent when I owned my agency. That was for everyday accounts my clients placed. If they had an account that was under $75 or over one year old, I charged a 50 percent commission. When I had a large client placing many accounts weekly or monthly, I would give them a special flat rate of 18 percent on all accounts across the board.

Some agencies will charge a flat monthly fee based on the number of accounts you place, how frequently you place them, the dollar amounts, and age. They also may charge per letter or per phone call and let you decide the frequency of each. Collection agencies may also offer other paid services at a flat fee. Check out their web sites and compare to see what the average fee structure is and what works for you and your business.

HOW USING A COLLECTION AGENCY AFFECTS SMALL BUSINESS OWNERS

If you decide to turn your delinquent accounts over to a collection agency, be prepared for the customer to call you. This doesn't always happen, but it has been my experience that they will call the business owner to try to work something out once the account has been placed with an agency. Once you place the account with an agency, all contacts must be referred back to the agency. If the debtor calls you, explain to them the account is with a collection agency and they have to call them. You can always brush off the discomfort of the call by saying, "My bookkeeper, accountant, (anyone but you) is handling my accounts and the policy is anything over 60 days is placed for collections." Once you hang up, e-mail or call your collection agency and let them know the debtor contacted you. If you receive mail or payments from the debtor, forward them to the agency.

Sometimes a customer will come back to you for services or products after they have paid a collection agency. Do not extend credit to this customer. Once you place an account with a collection agency, only accept cash payments up front. That customer cost you money when they didn't pay their bill, if they continue to purchase from you and have to pay cash, you might recoup your losses.

Using a collection agency can benefit your business because they save you time and money as well as the aggravation of making collection calls. They are specialized and trained in this type of work and may have tools and resources to help them collect quicker than you might be able to. There are also some other things to consider when using an agency—they do cost you money, you pay a fee on what they collect. You have to decide if that fee is worth the extra time and money you will have and the collection issues you will not have to deal with.

COLLECTION AGENCY PAYMENTS AND UPDATES

Most collection agencies send payments once a month and some twice a month. Quite a few agencies even offer online updates on the payments and status of your accounts that they are working on. You no longer have to wait a month to find out who paid; you can search online or even call for an update. Some business owners don't understand that when they place accounts with a collection agency, that does not guarantee the debt will be paid and the agency certainly never guarantees a time frame for it to be paid.

When I owned my agency I would have business owners place accounts with me and start calling me the next day to find out the status of the account and if it was paid. You have to remember, any money collected for you is money you thought you would not be able to collect without effort and time on your part. So, once you place accounts, give the agency some time to process and work on the account. Agencies also have to give the debtor 30 days by law to request verification of the debt and/or dispute the debt.

Most agencies have interactive web sites where you can look at your accounts, download reports and Excel spreadsheets, and sometimes even customize the reports.

CHAPTER 10

Fair Debt Collection Practices

WHAT IS THE FDCPA?

The Fair Debt Collections Practices Act (FDCPA) covers the collection practices of third-party debt collectors and attorneys who regularly collect debts for others. These laws also can affect business owners who do their own debt collections inhouse. Every business owner needs to be familiar with the FDCPA if they extend credit and will try to enforce their credit policy.

Business owners who grant credit should know this law because:

- Business owners' collection practices are covered by the law under certain conditions.
- Credit grantors should know what their collection services and attorneys may and may not do under the law, especially if they hire them to do collection work for them. Who you choose to do your collection work is a reflection of you and your business.
- Creditors may be liable with respect to the collection practices of third-party debt collectors under Section 5 of the Federal Trade Commission Act and in some cases under their state laws.
- Credit grantors must comply with FDCPA when they collect their own debts using a name other than their own. For example, Dunn's Oil Company uses the name The Dunn Collection Service to collect its own debts, so they must comply.

How do I create a solid customer base?

Having a credit policy and following the FDCPA weeds out the slow or nonpaying customers whom you don't want.

COMPLYING WITH THE FDCPA

A collector may communicate with the consumer or debtor between 8 a.m. and 9 p.m. local time of the consumer. If you know this is an inconvenient time for the consumer, you may set up another time for the communication. For example, if the consumer works third shift and tells you this so you can call when they are not working or sleeping, and you keep notes of this, you can call at that time even if it is not between 8 a.m. and 9 p.m.

If the customer notifies you or your collector in writing that they are refusing to pay and want you to stop calling or contacting them, you must stop communicating with them except to advise them of your possible actions because of this. These actions might be:

- That you are closing the account and won't continue to try to collect
- That you may take legal action
- That you may place the account with a collection agency
- That this may be reported to the credit bureau and affect their credit

When you are trying to collect on a debt you may not:

- Harass, oppress, or abuse the customer or debtor in any way. These words are not defined by the courts when cases arise under the law but this practice is not condoned by ethical businesses or collection agencies.
- Use any false or deceptive representations when trying to collect on accounts.
- Represent that you are affiliated with the United States government or any particular state government or that you are an attorney or work for a credit reporting agency if you don't.
- Threaten to take any action that is illegal or that you don't intend to take. This is why when you send a letter saying you will place an account with a collection agency in 15 days, you must follow through.
- Make a claim that the customer committed a crime by not paying their bill.
- Tell a customer or debtor that if they do not pay they will be arrested or imprisoned or that their property will be seized unless such action is legal and you intend to take it.

HOW THE FDCPA AFFECTS SMALL BUSINESS OWNERS

The FDCPA actually helps you have structure and rules for your credit policy. The FDCPA was created to protect consumers and became effective March 20, 1978. If you learn the FDCPA and follow it, you will see that you have much more success collecting from your customers. If you follow the guidelines and the law your business will be known as a fair, ethical, successful business and you will be known as a business owner who is serious about their business. Word gets around when you don't allow any slack with your payment terms and good business will attract good customers. Having a credit policy and following the FDCPA weeds out the slow or nonpaying customers whom you don't want. Personal, family, and household debts are covered under the Act. This includes money owed for the purchase of an automobile, for medical care, or for charge accounts. A debt collector is any person, other than the creditor, who regularly collects debts owed to others. Under a 1986 amendment to the Fair Debt Collection Practices Act, this includes attorneys who collect debts on a regular basis, but you should still be familiar with the Act. A collector may contact the consumer in person, by mail, telephone, telegram, or fax. However, a debt collector may not contact the consumer at unreasonable times or places, such as before 8 a.m. or after 9 p.m. (the consumer's time zone) unless the consumer agrees. A debt collector also may not contact the consumer at work if the collector knows that the consumer's employer disapproves.

CHAPTER 11

Cease and Desist: What Does It Mean?

EASE AND DESIST MEANS TO STOP. A debtor can send you, a collection agency, or anyone who is contacting them a letter asking them to cease and desist. If you receive a cease and desist letter you will want to place the account with an outside collection agency and let them know that you have received such a letter. You also could choose to hire an attorney or file a small claims action against them. Once you receive a letter asking you to cease and desist, your options are limited and you have to act quickly. By law, communication must stop at that time, except to notify the consumer of other legal actions you may take.

Most consumers do not realize that sending a cease and desist letter does not give them a free pass on paying for their debts. If they owe the money, they owe the money. The letter will only force the recip-

ient to take quicker, more drastic action. A cease and desist letter is designed for consumers who feel they are being harassed by a collector or collection agency. Consumers will send them out even when they are not being harassed; because they think it will stop the collection efforts and the debt will be dropped.

If you receive a cease and desist letter, you can only contact the debtor to let them know what action you will take, such as taking legal action or even closing the account.

BANKRUPTCY AND HOW IT AFFECTS SMALL BUSINESS OWNERS

There are three types of bankruptcy:

- Chapter 13—Wage earners, adjustment of debts of an individual with regular income

- Chapter 11—Business, reorganization
- Chapter 7—Total, liquidation

On April 20, 2005, President Bush signed into law the Bankruptcy Abuse Prevention and Consumer Protection Act of 2005. The BAPCPA has an impact on all small business owners and there are things you can do to protect your business.

Pay attention to your accounts receivables—you should review all accounts and watch larger accounts. If you are a very small business and losing one large account to a bankruptcy filing can upset your cash flow, you want to be on top of this. This is not to say your customers are all going to rush out and file bankruptcy but you need to watch accounts for signs that could lead to that.

Watch slow payers who suddenly place large orders. When a consumer or a business is anticipating financial trouble, they might try to stock up on your goods or services. Some things you can do if this happens is ask for a portion of the payment up front or ask that their balance be paid in full before another order is processed.

Some ways that the new law will help you is that you will find it easier to defend against a "preference" claim. The BAPCPA requires that any lawsuit to claw back a preference claim that's for less than $10,000 must be filed in the area where your business is located rather than in the city where the bankruptcy case or the consumer is located. This is great news for your business; you will not have to incur any costs by traveling or hiring an attorney in another state to defend the claim.

The BAPCPA also makes it easier for a business to defend itself against a preference claw back by eliminating the need to prove that the alleged preference payment was made in accord with "industry standards." Now the business will only need to prove that the payments were made in "the ordinary course of business" between the business and the bankrupt consumer or company.

The BAPCPA also gives you and your business 45 days to send a written demand for the return of your shipped goods if the customer files bankruptcy.

DEATH AND HOW IT AFFECTS SMALL BUSINESS OWNERS

When someone who owes money dies, their debts are paid out of their estate. A person's estate is made up of their money, including anything from insurance, property, investments, and possessions. Normally when someone dies if there is no will, someone, usually a relative, is appointed as the executor or administrator. A spouse is not automatically responsible for a spouse's debts, unless their name was on the note, it was a joint loan, or they provided a loan guarantee of some kind.

If there are debts owing at the time of death, the estate will pay off the debts owed in a specific order before any money goes to the people listed in the will. Most times personal loans or credit cards are paid last. Many times there is no money left for these types of bills.

If you have a lot of accounts extending credit to those who are elderly, or you offer a service to elderly people, this could be a concern for you and your business. You may want to take some precautions. Some things you could do are:

- Require two names on each account.
- Keep lower credit limits to reduce your risk.

- Only offer credit on one order at a time, meaning they would pay for one order before another could be charged.

Contact your insurance company to see if there are benefits to cover such situations.

When a customer dies, wait at least a month or more before contacting the family. Sometimes you may see the obituary in the paper or someone may tell you about the death. When I was the credit manager for an oil company we delivered fuel to a lot of local customers. I made it a point to read the obituaries every day. There is nothing worse than making a collection call and having a wife or family member, crying and upset, telling you that the person you want has died. You do have to stay on top of the situation if you want to eventually get paid, but use some tact.

Questions to ask when a debtor is deceased:

- Is there insurance?
- Who is the insurance company and what is their phone number?
- Who is handling the estate?

MY CUSTOMER SOLD OR WENT OUT OF BUSINESS

Some customers who go out of business will not file bankruptcy. If they file bankruptcy, you will receive paperwork in the mail about the proceedings and need to file a claim for what is owed to you. You cannot pursue the debt any other way and must wait until the court decides who gets paid what, if anything.

If a customer goes out of business and owes you money, you need to look at the paperwork and contracts you have with this customer. If they are going out of business, that means they do not have the money to operate day to day. Therefore they do not have the money to pay you. They might have to sell equipment to pay you or, if they signed a personal guarantee, you can ask them to pay you personally. If they sell their equipment, they will probably not get top dollar. It may take some time, and bills are paid in a specified order as outlined in the Bankruptcy Code.

CHAPTER 12

Fair Credit Reporting Act

WHAT IS THE FCRA?

THE FAIR CREDIT REPORTING ACT (FCRA) is enforced by the Federal Trade Commission and was designed to promote accuracy and ensure the privacy of the information used in consumer credit reports. This law, originally passed in 1970, ensures that consumers have access to information about them that lenders, insurers, and others obtain from credit bureaus and use to make decisions about providing credit and other services. The FCRA also requires that users of credit reports (this would be you or your business) have a "permissible purpose" to obtain them, and it also mandates that credit reporting agencies maintain the security and integrity of consumer files, and allows consumers to limit certain uses of their reports. Your "permissible purpose" would be to extend credit—thus the importance of a signed credit application.

The FCRA is made up of the following sections:

§ 601 Short title

§ 602 Congressional findings and statement of purpose

§ 603 Definitions; rules of construction

§ 604 Permissible purposes of consumer reports

§ 605 Requirements relating to information contained in consumer reports

§ 606 Disclosure of investigative consumer reports

§ 607 Compliance procedures

§ 608 Disclosures to governmental agencies

§ 609 Disclosures to consumers

§ 610 Conditions and form of disclosure to consumers

§ 611 Procedure in case of disputed accuracy

§ 612 Charges for certain disclosures

§ 613 Public record information for employment purposes

§ 614 Restrictions on investigative consumer reports

§ 615 Requirements on users of consumer reports

§ 616 Civil liability for willful noncompliance

§ 617 Civil liability for negligent noncompliance

§ 618 Jurisdiction of courts; limitation of actions

§ 619 Obtaining information under false pretenses

§ 620 Unauthorized disclosures by officers or employees

§ 621 Administrative enforcement

§ 622 Information on overdue child support obligations

§ 623 Responsibilities of furnishers of information to consumer reporting agencies

§ 624 Relation to state laws

§ 625 Disclosures to FBI for counterintelligence purposes

§ 626 Disclosures to governmental agencies for counterterrorism purposes

You can visit www.ftc.gov for more detailed information and also for a free written copy of the Act.

HOW THE FCRA AFFECTS SMALL BUSINESS OWNERS

When you decide to report debts to the various credit bureaus to affect a customer's credit, there are rules and laws you must follow. Violations of the FCRA can lead to both civil and criminal penalties. Civil penalties, including nominal damages (up to $1,000 if no actual damages exist), actual damages (including emotional distress), and punitive damages, plus attorneys' fees and costs, may apply where there is "willful noncompliance" with the Act. Civil penalties for "negligent noncompliance" are restricted to actual damages and attorneys' fees and costs. Criminal penalties may apply where an individual knowingly and willfully obtains information from a consumer reporting agency under false pretenses.

Employers and business owners who fail to give the appropriate notices or obtain authorizations may be sued by affected individuals. Consumer reporting agencies and users of consumer information who willfully or negligently fail to comply with any requirement imposed under the FCRA may be liable for actual damages, court costs, and reasonable attorneys' fees. Punitive damages also are available for willful violations. In addition, the FTC may sue employers for civil penalties of not more than $2,500 per violation.

The availability of tort actions by consumers is limited, however. The FCRA contains a provision that no consumer may bring any action or proceeding for defamation, invasion of privacy, or negligence with respect to the reporting of information against any consumer reporting agency, any user of information (including employers or perspective employers), or any person who furnishes information to a consumer reporting agency unless the information is false and has been provided with malice or willful intent to injure the consumer. I cannot stress this enough—make sure you have all documentation and that you have signed copies.

COMPLYING WITH THE FCRA

The FCRA imposes specific restrictions and obligations on any employer's use of consumer reporting agencies and consumer reports.

Disclosure and Authorization Required for Consumer Reports

Before you can obtain a consumer credit report, you must disclose to that person in writing that such a report may be obtained and secure the person's written authorization. This written disclosure must be contained in a separate document used *solely* for that purpose, and it may not simply be included on an employment application or in an employee handbook. This is why I suggest you add this to your credit applications and new account forms.

Additional Disclosure Required for Investigative Consumer Reports

If you wish to obtain an investigative consumer report for a new employee, you *must* follow the requirements discussed above with respect to consumer reports *and* meet the following additional requirements:

- You must advise the employee or applicant in writing that an investigative consumer report may be requested no later than three days after the report is requested.
- You must advise the employee or applicant that the report may include information as to his/her character, general reputation, and personal characteristics.
- You must provide the individual with a summary of his/her rights under the FCRA.

Visit www.ftc.gov for sample forms and letters.

If you wish to order an investigative consumer report you must advise the potential employee that, on written request, you will provide additional information, including a "complete and accurate disclosure of the nature and scope of the investigation requested." If the additional disclosure is requested by the potential employee within a "reasonable period of time," this information must be provided by the employer (you) in writing and delivered (personally or by mail) no later than five days after receipt of the request or five days after the report is ordered, whichever is later. I would suggest using certified mail or a delivery confirmation service. Before taking any "adverse action" (which includes "a denial of employment or any other decision for employment purposes that adversely affects a current or prospective employee") based in whole or in part on a consumer report, you must provide the affected person with a copy of the report and a written description of that person's rights under the FCRA. (The consumer reporting agency must include the description of rights with the consumer report. The appropriate information is also included in an FTC publication entitled, "A Summary of Your Rights under the FCRA.") Visit the web site of the agency you pull the report from for a sample of what to send.

If you take any adverse action, you again must notify the consumer that adverse action has been taken based in whole or in part on a consumer report. Then you must provide the individual with:

- The name, address, and telephone number

of the reporting agency (including the toll-free number of a national agency);

- The notice of their right to obtain an additional free copy of the report by making the request within 60 days;
- A notice of the person's right to dispute the accuracy or completeness of the report with the consumer reporting agency; and
- A notice that the consumer reporting agency did not make the decision to take the adverse action and is unable to provide the person the specific reasons why the action was taken. They should contact you for this information.

This is similar to the information you must include in the letter when someone is denied credit.

The Federal Trade Commission (FTC) has taken the position that the legislative history of the FCRA clearly anticipates that this notice will be accompanied by an opportunity to clear up any errors in the report, and the FCRA contains comprehensive procedures whereby consumers can correct such errors through the credit reporting agency. The FCRA, however, does not require employers to refrain from taking any action based on a negative report once the notice has been given. Nor does it require employers to give applicants or employees an opportunity to respond or explain, or to alter a decision based on an incorrect report. Furthermore, employers are excluded from liability based on any error in a consumer report provided by a consumer reporting agency.

Before a consumer reporting agency may provide or prepare a consumer report for an employer, it must obtain certification from the employer that the employer (1) provided the required disclosure to the applicant/employee, (2) received written permission to obtain the report, (3) will not use the information in violation of any applicable equal employment opportunity law or regulation, and (4) will abide by the requirements stated before taking any adverse employment action. So before you try to obtain a credit report for employment purposes make sure you have all the documentation you need and that it is signed by the potential employee.

HANDLING REPORTED DISPUTES

Once you begin reporting debts to the credit bureaus you will sometimes receive a notice in the mail from the credit bureau that something you included in a person's credit report is being disputed by that consumer. You will need to verify the reported information and sometimes be required to provide backup documentation to support your information. This could be proof of the debt or verification, such as purchase orders, proof of delivery, signed contracts or agreements, or copies of statements and invoices.

WHAT IS CREDIT REPORTING?

Credit reporting is a report documenting the credit history and current status of a borrower's credit standing. Credit reporting is something business owners do to show when they have customers who have paid on time or are past due. Most businesses only report negative experiences, but you can and should also report positive payment histories. This can also be used as a great customer service tool. When you report that someone has always made payments on time, send a letter or note to that customer letting them know this. They will appreciate this and it can prompt them to refer you to other potential customers, purchase more from you, and ensure they will stay a good loyal customer for many more years to come.

When you report negative payment histories, it is mostly used as a tool to get those clients to pay. If you affect their ability to obtain credit from someone else, they may pay you on time to maintain or correct a poor credit report.

CAN A SMALL BUSINESS OWNER DO THEIR OWN CREDIT REPORTING?

Absolutely! When you sign up with one of the three credit bureaus, tell them what services you require. You may want to pull reports to check credit, screen potential employees, and report delinquent payments. Each one of these things is a different service that you pay for with each bureau. So be clear as to what you want when you sign up with them to ensure you get all the tools you need to have a sound credit policy in place.

Some tools the credit bureaus can provide you with are listed below. Remember, you will probably have to pay a fee for any of these services and they vary from credit bureau to credit bureau, so check out each credit bureau and choose the one that has the tools you need most at the best price. They also may offer small business package deals at a discounted rate.

- Bankruptcy alerts—These match bankruptcy, dismissal, and discharge filings to a customer's base or portfolio. You are notified of the bankruptcy usually within 72 hours of public availability. This alert delivers valuable information throughout the filing's life cycle—such as new filings, changes to the filing, dismissals, and discharges all in an easy-to-use electronic format.

- Small business account triggering—Have your small business accounts monitored and receive notification when new derogatory information on one of your customers has been recorded in the Small Business Enterprise databases, enabling you to take timely action to reduce losses.

HOW TO DO CREDIT REPORTING

When you sign up and sit down to start your first batch of credit reporting, you will probably be at your computer. You can now report online 24/7 with most bureaus and it is instantly transmitted to them. Following is a list of some information you will need to start reporting debts.

- Full name
- Address
- Social security number
- Date of birth
- Original creditor, if different from yourself
- Date of original order
- Due date
- Amount past due and how many days it is past due

If you do not have all of this information, such as a social security number, you can still report the debt. The bureau will use what information you do provide to locate the correct report. The more thorough your information, the easier for them to locate the report and the sooner it is reflected on the report. So try to have as much information as possible, but do not withhold reporting on someone because you do not have "enough" information.

When you sign up with your agency, they will give you a user name and password so you can log in to their web site. A form will come up asking you for information that you just type in. Hit the Submit button and you are done. You can do your reporting as it happens, once a month, once a week, or whatever works for you. Remember, once you report a delinquent debt, if you receive any payments, report them immediately.

Some software programs have credit reporting included as part of the program, which makes it easy to report with just a mouse click.

TO WHOM DO I REPORT?

You can report to one, two, or all three of the credit bureaus. The contact information for all three bureaus follows.

Equifax Credit Information Services, Inc.
P.O. Box 740241
Atlanta, GA 30374
Call 1-888-202-4025
www.equifax.com

Experian
www.experian.com
Call 888-243-6951

TransUnion
P.O. Box 2000
Chester, PA 19022
www.transunion.com

They all offer different service packages and pricing. You don't have to report to all three—you can report to one, two, or all of them. It is up to you and your budget.

PART V

What Makes a Successful Credit Policy?

CHAPTER 13

Reasons to Implement a Credit Policy

IF YOU HAVE READ THIS FAR, YOU NOW know how important a credit policy is to your business's success. If you still think you don't need a credit policy, here are some highlights of why it is so very important to have a sound credit policy in place.

- A credit policy will provide timely notification to your customers regarding any past due amounts, therefore eliminating old balances from being carried on the receivables.
- A credit policy will outline a procedure that will provide your customers with options when they cannot pay in full or on time.
- A credit policy will provide a procedure on when and what to do with small balances on customers' accounts.
- A credit policy will provide a procedure that will enable you to adequately provide reasonable credit limits for customers with revolving credit.
- A credit policy will provide guidelines to legally collect money due to your company that was lost because of bad checks.
- A credit policy will provide you with a system that will maintain timely contact with your customers when they are past due. It also will provide a procedure that will enable your business to keep credit card numbers and checking account information on file for customers and automatically charge them when they place an order or for scheduled monthly or weekly payments.
- A credit policy will enable your business to be aware of when an account should be placed for collection and to avoid carrying bad debts on the receivables.

- A credit policy will provide you with a procedure that will eliminate orders being held for nonpayment and will better serve customers in a timely manner.
- A credit policy will enable you to be aware of when to write off a balance to bad debt.

As I stated in Chapter 5, it is not just important for you to understand your credit policy, it is also very important for your customers and employees to understand it as well. It is your job to educate your customers and employees on your credit policy in order for it to work well for you and your customers. It is important that your customers know your credit policy and/or terms of payment before they ever start doing business with you. Reiteration of your credit policy, every chance you get, is a good business practice to get into.

Make sure your credit policy covers the following:

- How to apply for credit (using a credit application)
- Late fees, interest fees, collection, court or bad check fees
- Repayment terms and conditions
- Credit limits
- Buyer responsibilities
- Seller liability

THINGS ENTREPRENEURS SHOULD AVOID WHEN EXTENDING CREDIT

Any new business owner should avoid opening any account for any new customer without having them fill out a credit application. This is harder than you think. You will get potential customers that say, "Oh, I have plenty of money," or "I work at so-and-so and make huge amounts of money so I don't need to fill that out." Tell them it is a policy and you have to have it to establish a credit limit or they must pay cash. This is the biggest problem most business owners have, right in the beginning. They do not want to ask for the form to be filled out or they don't want to push the issue. Remember, if someone does not want to fill out a credit application, *there is a reason*. If they fill it out happily, they are "usually" credit approved. Be very aware of this and get a signed credit application for every customer with whom you do business.

When you are checking a customer's credit, look for things such as how long they have been in business or have lived at the same address. Check their credit report for payment information, judgments, bankruptcies, liens, lawsuits, corporate records, or fictitious business name filings. Always call the credit references they provide you with, but remember, they chose those references. Be sure to call some of their suppliers and their bank for a clearer picture.

Some warning signs to look for are:

- Does the company offer large discounts or sales frequently? If they do, they might not be making enough money to be able to pay you.
- Does the company have accounts with your competition and is it possibly overextended? Sometimes someone will apply for credit at competitors because they owe the original creditor money and their account is shut off.
- Has the company or potential customer already used property or assets as collateral for another loan?
- Is their income seasonal?

TOP 11 WEB SITES FOR SMALL BUSINESS OWNERS AND ENTREPRENEURS

Credit and Collections

www.credit-and-collections.com

This is my free e-mail list for businesspeople and people in the credit and collections field. When you join, you get to share ideas, information, and network with other large and small business owners, entrepreneurs, and very knowledgeable people in the credit and collections field. You get free information for your business, free promotion for your business, and a lot of free tools and forms.

Home Business Magazine

www.homebusinessmag.com

An international publication, available on newsstands, in bookstores, via subscription, and online. *Chock full* of helpful information for anyone starting a new business or running an existing business.

Entrepreneur

www.entrepreneur.com

This web site offers subscriptions to their popular magazine, many business books, including books like this one in their Ultimate Series, information on starting your business, marketing, growing, business plans, how to's, franchises, raising money, and so much more.

More Business

www.morebusiness.com

This web site offers sample business plans, sample contracts, and information on small business marketing.

Internal Revenue Service

www.irs.gov/businesses/small

If you're considering starting a business, start here. This section of their web site provides information such as a checklist for a new business and how to select a business structure. Learn about operating a business with employees, deductions and credits, recordkeeping and accounting methods. Additional resources include the Small Business Tax Calendar, Tax Topics for Businesses, and Frequently Asked Questions.

Business Info Guide

www.businessinfoguide.com

Resources and industry information for entrepreneurs. This site includes industry-specific information, business startup checklists and tools, resources for all 50 states, articles from small business experts, and more.

Ms. Financial Savvy

www.msfinancialsavvy.com

This site is geared toward women, but anyone can visit and benefit from the resources found here. This is a vast web site of much educational and informative information. Learn about small business, investing, mutual funds, stock market investing, retirement planning, home mortgages, scholarships, budget travel, saving money, and more.

United States Small Business Association

www.sba.gov

This site maintains and strengthens the nation's economy by aiding, counseling, assisting, and protecting the interests of small businesses. Visit this site for information on business development, financing a business, research, starting your business, and more.

My Business

www.mybusinessmag.com

My Business magazine's 600,000 subscribers are members of the National Federation of Independent Business (NFIB), the largest business advocacy group in the United States.

Inc.com

www.inc.com/home

The resource for growing companies. This site has so many articles and tips for you and your business; you also can sign up for a free daily e-mail of top news stories.

Startup Journal

www.startupjournal.com

The *Wall Street Journal* center for entrepreneurs includes articles, business plan tools, trademark research, a bookstore, and a discussion area with free networking.

TIPS TO GET YOUR BUSINESS OUT OF DEBT

If you do not have a credit policy and you extend credit, you will end up in debt. You will not have the cash flow you need to pay your bills and build good credit for your business.

One of the most common things small business owners do to get out of debt is to raise their prices or add another service without incurring more costs. If you have not raised your prices lately or at all this is an easy way to get back on track fairly quickly. You also can create another service that won't cost a lot to implement; for instance, when I had my collection agency, I created a letter service. I just had to create three letters and a web page to advertise this. You could hang a sign in your office, run a small ad in a local paper, or put the information on your invoices or statements, so it goes out with your regular mailings and lets your existing customers know you have a new service.

> Neither a borrower nor a lender be.
>
> *—Shakespeare, Hamlet, I, iii*

Don't keep a high level of inventory—sell all you can so you will have less money tied up. Send out invoices immediately; do not wait. Send them out early and often. Don't try to grow your business when you are trying to create more cash flow, just try to maintain until you are out of debt. Don't pay your bills as they arrive in your office, check the terms. If you don't get a discount for paying early, don't. Don't spend any extra money until your debt is gone, and don't use credit cards. Use your debit card or checks for things you must have and for normal everyday business expenses. Only spend money you have. Some business owners will go without a salary to save money for their business. If you don't want to go without a salary, make sure yours is not extravagant. Recycle and conserve, with paper, folders, boxes, packing materials.

FIVE WAYS TO BETTER BUSINESS CREDIT

1. Have a Business Plan with a Credit Policy. When you create a business plan to try and get a loan from a bank to finance your startup business, be sure to include a credit policy. This will show any bank that you have already thought ahead and planned on how to keep your cash flow steady and pay your bills, including theirs. When you start any business, there are three plans you need:

- Business Plan
- Credit and Collections Plan
- Marketing Plan

If you have these three plans, you will have a direct path to success. You may change some things on them as you go, but the direction is there. Having a streamlined plan that works with your other plans almost guarantees your success. Sometimes I get so far ahead in a plan, and things start happening so fast, that I think I am following my plan too quickly. Sometimes I have to wait days or months before taking a next step on my plan. You will see, once you follow your plans for what to do each day as you run your business, you will notice you get pretty busy, and sometimes have to wait to get back to the next item in your plan. This is all part of your road to success.

2. Set Your Pricing Correctly. If you set the price of your service or items in the correct way to make you money and not cost you money (many businesses do this!) you should not have a problem. I have found some new business owners will set a price so low they are not making any money; they are barely covering expenses and not making a profit. One of the reasons they have given me for doing this is, "This is what the competition charges." This may be a huge company that can afford to charge such a low price. You should check out more than what they charge—check out their turnaround time, their customer serv-

ice, their hours. See what they are lacking and add that to your slogan and you will gain customers, even if your price is higher because you are giving them something that may be important to them that they can't get at the competition's. Perhaps offer outstanding customer service, or maybe free delivery. Find out what the competition is not doing, and do it.

3. Offer Discounts and Take Early Pay Discounts. If you have a credit policy, you may be offering discounts to some customers, maybe for orders above a certain dollar amount or an early payment discount. This helps you to get paid larger sums of money quicker, therefore allowing you to take advantage of early pay discounts.

4. Send Out Invoices and Statements in a Timely Fashion. If you are not prompt with sending out your invoices and statements, you will send the message that getting paid is not that important to you. This tells your customers that they also can take their time when paying you. When you send a bill immediately after a service or product is delivered, you are telling that customer, thank you for your business, I did my part of the deal, now its time for you to do yours.

5. Check Credit and Enforce Credit Limits. You can only set credit limits if you check credit. So if you are extending credit, you have to make sure you don't extend too much credit. For example, someone who seems to only be able to pay off a $500-a-month bill maybe should have a credit limit of only $500 or less. If their limit is $1,000 they could end up owing you $500 to $1,000 every month. This would impair your cash flow, making you less money, therefore not allowing you to pay your bills or take a pre-payment discount.

To avoid running your business aground in debt, ask yourself these questions:

- How much volume of products or services can you realistically sell in the next year?
- How much will you charge for your goods or services? Should you raise your rates?
- How much will it cost to produce your product or update your services?
- How much are your monthly operating expenses?
- Do you need to hire employees? If so, how many, and how much will you pay them?
- How much will you pay yourself?
- How much payroll tax, unemployment tax, and workers' compensation will you pay?
- Can and are you offering employee benefits and how much does that cost you?

Once you have the answers to these questions you will be able to figure out how much money you need to make each month in order to run your business and make a profit.

CHAPTER 14

Helpful Collection Tips

O NE OF THE THINGS I AM MOST asked about is tips for doing debt collection. The most popular is telephone collections tips. I have tried to compile many of the excuses I have been given, and what a good response would be, as well as tips to get the debtor to give you more information that will help with the collection call and dunning letters.

COLLECTION CALL TELEPHONE TIPS

Making collection calls is an art. You need to anticipate what the customer is going to say and be ready for anything. You have to stay in control of the phone call.

Making collection calls to your customers has some advantages. They are:

- Inexpensive—compared to personal visits and individually typed letters.
- Immediate—produces some sort of answer the moment the contact is made.
- Personal—allows an exchange between two people.
- Informative—allows you to ask questions, obtain information, and take appropriate action.
- Flexible—approach can be varied as changing situations demand.

For your collection call to be a success it must always result in agreement as to what is to be done. Following are some things you can do to get your collection calls to bring you results.

Use voice mail or answering machines if available. Leave detailed and complete messages, speak slowly and always tell them what you want them to do, such as to please return your call by a certain time or day. Don't leave an open-ended message that just says you called, but not why, or what you want them to do.

Always be courteous.

If you speak with a secretary or spouse, you can tell them you are calling in regard to an invoice, rather than a debt.

Create a sense of urgency by leaving a deadline time to hear from them, whether you speak with a person or leave a message on a machine.

Get the name of the person in charge of issuing checks or paying bills.

Ask for the best time to call them in the future.

Get the name of the person answering your call. If you don't get a call back, ask for that person when you call again. When you speak to the person you are trying to get hold of, you can tell them, "I left four messages with Susie—didn't she give them to you?" This sometimes gets the person to call you back in the future so as not to make the message taker look bad. The most important things to remember when making collection calls are to get or confirm the name of the person in charge of paying invoices. Try to find out the best time to reach the person you are calling, leave your complete name, company name, phone number, and a request for a call back if you get a person taking a message. Leave the same information on voice mail. Always get the name of the person taking the message and ask the person taking the message when the person you need can be reached.

Do not make a demand for payment if you are speaking with a receptionist or someone else who is not involved with paying the bills. If you are asked the purpose of your call, simply state that it is in reference to an invoice or their account. Create a sense of urgency by giving a time you need a call back by. Always be courteous and professional. Use voice mail effectively if available.

Leave a detailed, complete message and be sure to speak clearly and slowly. Include your phone number, e-mail, and a time by which you would like a return call.

COMMON DEBT COLLECTION ERRORS

If you are creating your credit policy and just starting out, you may not be familiar with some common errors or mistakes business owners make when collecting on past due accounts. I have listed some of the most common here for you. Make sure you don't make these mistakes.

- Not checking customers' credit history before extending credit.
- Not getting a credit application, agreement, or contract in writing and signed.
- Not being familiar with the FDCPA and unintentionally "harassing" a debtor.
- Overlooking small balances.
- Not asking for the money that is owed because they hate asking for money.
- Not knowing when it is the right time to turn a debt over to a collection agency.
- Not having a credit policy in place and enforcing it.
- Extending credit to anyone who walks in the door or calls on the phone because they "sound like they will pay."
- Not taking action on NSF notices or bad checks.
- Not using letters and forms to collect on past due accounts.
- Not having a credit application.
- Not pulling credit reports and checking references.

- Not understanding how to communicate with customers so they stay current.
- Not having a budget and controlling cash flow.
- Not knowing how to effectively do business online.
- Not using small claims court to their advantage.
- Not using discounts and incentives to persuade customers to pay early.
- Not educating themselves with online resources and networking groups.
- Not understanding how a collection agency can work for them.
- Not knowing how to set up realistic payment arrangements with customers.
- Not knowing what to do if a customer dies or files for bankruptcy.
- Not training oneself or staff.
- Waiting too long to use a collection agency.

If you are aware of these common mistakes you can take steps to avoid them and keep them from happening to you and your business. Reading this book and using the tools I am sharing with you will help you to do this.

How to Correct Debt Collection Errors

- Enforce your credit policy.
- Make sure your debtor is "worth" something before suing them—if they don't have any assets there is nothing to attach or garnish if they do not pay.
- Ask for payment when payment is due.

- Research and sign up with a collection agency even before you need one, and then place accounts before they are too old.

I recently read an article about a "bust out" scheme that defrauded creditors. A company (that had a credit policy in place) received a credit application and an order from a corporation requesting a moderate six-figure credit limit. The company checked the references listed on the credit application and they were unverifiable. Also, the corporation was related to one of the references where previous collection attempts had been unsuccessful. One reference did not have a physical address and the phone number given was that of the owner of the corporation. Another reference had never heard of the corporation. Another reference was a business that was not related to the same industry. The company tried to fax the remaining references but never heard back from any of them. After much research it was found that this corporation had created a "bust out" scheme to defraud vendors out of at least $2 million in cash, credit, or merchandise.

Always check credit references. If something doesn't seem right, it's probably not. If you are not happy with the references provided to you, ask for additional references. This customer wants credit from you, so you call the shots. If you give them credit without checking them out, they call the shots. The only way to keep control of your money is to have a credit policy in place. Why would you let anyone else control your cash flow?

TOP DEBTOR EXCUSES FOR NOT PAYING AND HOW TO HANDLE THEM

Consumer Excuses

- Upon receipt of my telephone call inquiring about payment of my bill one customer said, "We didn't budget for you this year!" Immediately find your signed order, agreement, or contract and start vigorous collection efforts. Also, revoke their credit.
- "The check is in the mail." Great! Ask, "When did you mail the check? What was the check amount? What address did you mail it to? What is the check number? When is the check dated?"
- "I already paid." Follow with: "When did you pay? Did you pay by check, money order, credit card? How much was the payment for?" Ask for a copy of the receipt or cancelled check.
- "I don't have any money." Oh. Ask, "How are you paying your rent, phone bill, etc.? Can you borrow money from someone? Can you pay with a credit card?"
- "I'm divorced and my ex is supposed to pay that bill." Ask them to send you a copy of the divorce decree that states this.
- "There was a problem with the service, product etc." Immediately ask, "Why didn't you call or tell me three months ago when you discovered this problem?" Check their contract or order—did they have 30 days to dispute or is it open-ended?
- "I am sick and have medical bills." Ask, "Do you have insurance?" Set up a payment plan.
- "I don't have a job." Ask, "Are you getting unemployment checks? Is your spouse working? Are you looking for a job? Anything promising?" Call back on the day they tell you they might have a job interview to see how it went.
- "My wife (husband) handles that." Find out who ordered the product or service or who signed the contract. Ask, "When will your husband or wife be home? Do they have a work or cell number I can call?"
- "I'll try to make a payment." Ask, "How? What is your plan?"
- "You're harassing me!" Ask, "How?" Explain the details of payments and try to set up a payment plan.
- "I'll pay in full when I get my tax refund, insurance settlement, Christmas club money, etc." Ask, "How much is your refund for? When did you send in your taxes? Who did your taxes?"
- "Hold on a minute," and then they disconnect you! Immediately call back and leave a message then send a follow-up letter.
- "I can't get a loan." Reply by asking, "Can you borrow from family or friends? Can you pay with a credit card?" Try to set up a payment plan.
- "My insurance company should have paid that." Ask for documentation stating this. "Who is your insurance company? What is their number? Who should I talk to there?"
- "When I have some extra money I will pay you." Ask how they will have extra money.
- "I have more important bills to pay." Explain what will happen if they don't pay, such as this being reported to the credit bureau, credit being revoked, or anything

else you may have to do to enforce payment.

- When the person you are calling is not at home, ask when they will be home. Call back at that time.

Commercial Excuses

- "We're filing for bankruptcy." Ask for paperwork, attorney's name, address, and phone number, then call the attorney.
- "Your invoice has to be approved by another department." Ask which department. Ask for a contact name and number, call them and state that "Bob" said you are the person who handles this.
- "We're waiting for our customers to pay us." Send them a copy of my book, *Become the Squeaky Wheel*, explain that their customers' not paying them is not your problem and you need to get paid or credit will be revoked.
- "We did not receive the product (service)." Get proof of delivery and send it to them; follow up with a call.
- "The check is waiting to be signed." Ask who signs the checks. Get the name and number of that person and ask to be transferred. Call that person until you get an answer.
- "We did not receive an invoice, statement, etc." E-mail or fax the invoice and call right back.
- "There's something wrong with the product." Check your contract—did they have 30 days to report this?
- "The bookkeeper is sick or on vacation."

Ask who pays the bills when they are gone. Speak to that person.

- "The computer is down." Call back in an hour.
- "You're not on my list." E-mail or fax the invoice and call right back.
- "Accounts Payable only takes calls on Tuesdays between 1 and 3." Call back at that time.

Funniest and Strangest Excuses

Following are some actual excuses that I have received from debtors while making collection calls.

- "I lost my glasses and couldn't read my mail."
- "My car is broken down and the nearest mailbox is ten miles away!"
- "That person is deceased," and a week later at the same phone number, "that person is not home right now!"
- "I didn't know I had to actually pay that bill."
- "I was robbed of my mail at the Post Office while trying to mail your check. When I got home I couldn't find my checkbook. As soon as I find my checkbook I will send your check."

SILENCE IS GOLDEN

My favorite tool when making collection calls is silence. I had read about this in books and had other collectors tell me about it, and it is really hard to do. Once you do it and get good at it, you will always do it. It works great. Just call your debtor and explain why you are calling as I have mentioned earlier and then just wait for a response. I have had debtors just sit and watch TV; I can hear the TV in the background and they just don't say anything because they really don't know what to say. I have had to say, "Hello? Are you there?" They reply, "Yes." I repeat who I am and why I am calling, and ask the question again. I have had debtors hang up on me, or just swear at me. I have had some tell me their life story of why they can't pay, and others go on and on but make the payment or a payment arrangement.

> **I often regret that I have spoken; never that I have been silent.**
>
> *—Publibius Syrus Moral Sayings, 1st Cent. BCE*

When you make collection calls and deal with debtors, you might need to brush up on some people skills. I have attended seminars on telephone collections and read books about them as well as books about dealing with difficult people, anger management, psychology, and mediation skills. These are all tools you will need when dealing with a client or customer who has become past due and is unable or unwilling to pay.

I find these tools helpful when performing customer service and networking as well. The more you know about your potential customers and how to handle what their needs are, the more success you will have.

TIPS FOR IMPROVING YOUR COLLECTION PROCEDURES

Some businesses have slow-paying customers or past due balances because they didn't "train" their customers in the beginning. It is important that your customers know your credit policy and/or terms of payment *before* they become customers. Reiteration of your credit policy, when payment is overdue, is a good step to take in trying to obtain payment. Always ask for payment when it is justly due.

You should never extend credit to a new customer without having them complete a credit application and go through the credit approval policy. Once you extend credit, it is important to maintain accurate records on an account payment history.

Adhere to your collection policies no matter what. You cannot see the future or changing market conditions. Try to keep current with trade reports pertaining to specific companies and industries.

Change your collection letters frequently—you can make them stronger and more action-oriented.

Discourage payments on account or changes in payment terms. Too many payment plans or changed payment terms can impair your cash flow.

When you receive payments "on account" be sure to follow up right away with a letter or phone call thanking them for their payment and telling them what their new balance is and when to send the next payment. Don't ask them when they will send the payment, tell them when to send it.

On large accounts call or send a reminder just a few days after terms if they become delinquent.

Ask to speak to a manager or owner when making collection calls rather than speaking to a secretary or receptionist. Go right for the decision maker.

If a customer disputes the quality of merchandise or service, price or delivery, you should attempt to resolve this right away. Insist they pay the portion of the bill that they are not disputing while you work out the disputed problem.

If all else has failed, you may want to refer the account to an outside collection agency.

Update your records often, making sure the telephone numbers you have and addresses for your customers are current and up to date.

PART VI

Cash Management and Maximizing Cash Flow

CHAPTER 15

Assessing Your
Cash Position

ASSESSING YOUR CASH POSITION IS
realizing your cash flow, and
knowing what you have for cash.
How do you know if you are
making money? How much extra money
do you have? What should you do with it?
Some new business owners will see that
money is coming in, bills are getting paid,
and things seem to be flowing smoothly.
When this happens, you cannot just sit
back and expect everything to keep flowing smoothly. You need to be sure your
collections, billing, and payments and
accounts payables are all working for you.
Good records provide the financial data
that help you operate more efficiently,
which increases your profitability.
Accurate and complete records enable you
and/or your accountant to identify all
your business assets, liabilities, income,
and expenses. That information, when

compared to appropriate industry aver-
ages, helps you pinpoint both the strong
and weak phases of your business opera-
tions. Good records are essential for the
preparation of current financial statements, such as the income statement
(profit and loss) and cash-flow projection.
These statements, in turn, are critical for
maintaining good relations with your
bank, accountant, and the IRS. As you
know, good records are extremely important at tax time.

If you do not know or do not want to
learn the basic principles of accounting,
you will need to hire an accountant. This
will be money well spent if you are not
familiar with bookkeeping and taxes. You
also will have one less job, meaning one
less thing to stress over when you outsource your bookkeeping to an accountant
or hire a bookkeeper to do this for you.

PAYING YOUR BILLS ON TIME OR EARLY

Remember to invoice clients immediately, get as many up-front payments as possible, and hold onto your money as long as possible when paying your bills. Pay your bills when they are due or early if they offer you a discount. Pay them on time so you do not incur any late fees. If you end up with extra cash you may want to invest it somewhere or even invest it back into your business. Some business owners hire an accountant or lawyer to handle this aspect of their business and some do it themselves. You want to use your excess cash to improve your company's stability. You may have a business loan to pay down—pay it off early. Be sure to check your contract to see if there is a pre-payment penalty.

Some things you can do to make bill paying easier are to make a special place just for your bills; a drawer, a folder, or a box. When your bills arrive, open them and put them in this special place, then when you are ready to pay your bills, they will all be together. Based on the due dates listed on your bills choose a time twice a month to pay bills—this could be the beginning or end of the month. Some people pay their bills in the middle of the month. Choose the time that works best for you and your bills.

Sometimes you can call your suppliers and ask to have your due date changed, to the end of the month or the beginning; that way all your bills can be due around the same time. Write the due date of your bills on your calendar, or use your computer's calendar. I use the reminder service in Outlook to alert me when a bill is due or when I have an appointment. This way you will not miss any payments. Another method to keep track of your bills is a tickler file. To do this, you set up hanging file folders 1 through 31 and January through December. Rotate the folders as the day and month come up. Place your bills in the folder for the day you need to pay it, or a few days before. Remember to allow for mailing days. If you receive a bill a couple of months ahead of time, you can put it into the next month's folder and switch it to the "day" folder once next month is here.

Try to pay your bills with a check so you have a record of the payment. Put the bills for which you have written checks in a pile, with stamps on them near your car keys. This way you will remember to mail them when you leave your office. Some of your suppliers may offer online bill payment options—try to take advantage of this if possible and save on envelopes and stamps.

IMPROVING CASH FLOW

To improve your cash flow, you have already taken the first step by reading this book. Most entrepreneurs do not think about credit policies or debt collection when they think about improving their cash flow. I have always seen any amount outstanding, where the service has already been provided, as an avenue for improving my cash flow. This money is owed to you, and you need to ask for it and get it, improving your cash flow immediately. Implementing a credit policy then allows for this outstanding amount to be smaller, thus improving your cash flow.

If you need more money for your business, look at your accounts receivable report. If you have 1,000 customers who owe you $500 that is over 60 days past due, sit down, pick up the phone, and spend a couple of hours calling them. Even if you leave messages and don't get a live person, you will see some checks in a few days and you also could get some immediate payments over the phone. A couple of hours well spent.

Another way to improve cash flow is by taking any discounts offered to you by your suppliers. If a supplier offers you a discount to pay in 15 days rather than the net 30, depending on how much you spend with them, that could be a good amount of money. If you take advantage of that discount every month for a year, it can add up, improving your cash flow.

Check your invoices. Mistakes can happen and some businesses find errors up to 5 percent on their billings—this can add up. Be sure you are billed at the price you were quoted, that the sales tax is correct, or the shipping fees are what you agreed on.

This includes your utility bills. Do you pay a water bill? How is your plumbing? Is it leaking? If it is, this could be costing you money. The same with your electric bills—How old is your wiring? Things that are repaired and running efficiently will save you money in the long run. Try to do maintenance regularly to save money. Look into the best plan for your phone service; call your phone company or research online before you call. Find out what things you need for your business and see if they have a plan that includes just those features. So many times we end up paying for things we don't need or use. Ask yourself how many phone lines you need, if you need caller ID, voice mail, how many voice mailboxes, and what kind of long-distance service you need. You get the idea—if they don't have a package that includes just what you need, ask them if they can create

one.

Keep track of the money you spend and re-evaluate it. For example, do you buy your employees lunch every day? Maybe you could cut this back to only on Fridays, or buy them coffee instead. Another example might be if you spend quite a bit on different training seminars, maybe you could get someone to come to your office and have a seminar that everyone can benefit from all at once, which would be much cheaper.

Look at your business; are you spending money on things to make an appearance? Quite a few new business owners want to look immediately successful and will spend so much money on glossy expensive brochures, or brand new fancy furniture when they haven't gotten to the point where they can really afford it yet. I still work at a desk I purchased at a second-hand shop for $100.

Another way you can increase cash flow is to figure out what your everyday business bills total for the year. For example, figure out how much your electric, Internet, phone, and water bills were for the past year. Did your electric bill go up over the year? Did your phone bill increase? If so, look at the bills and figure out why. Do you have faulty wiring that could be fixed and therefore save you money on your electric bill? Do you let employees use your business line to make long-distance calls? Maybe you need to look at your long-distance service and research a new carrier. This can take some initial time but can save you a lot of money in the long run and in the coming year. Check out your insurance options. Can you find an agent who will cover your business insurance and vehicle insurance for a lower rate? Check your suppliers' invoices—what are you paying for shipping? Is there a cheaper shipping method you could use? If you find a cheaper supplier or a cheaper shipping rate, ask your current supplier if they can match it. They may do this if not doing so means losing you as a customer.

Another tip is to send your invoice with your product if this is feasible. Sometimes you can't do this if the billing address is different from the shipping address, but if it is all going to the same place anyway, send the invoice with the product. Check out what you are paying for advertising. Do you still need to advertise so much? Can you advertise cheaper? Once you get your business up and running you may be able to cut out advertising altogether. Be sure you aren't wasting money on advertising that isn't doing anything for you.

WATCHING YOUR OVERHEAD

What is overhead? In a business, it is the expenses and costs that are not directly associated with the production or sale of goods and services. These are the normal costs of being in business, such as office rent, utilities, insurance, advertising, accounting, and legal expenses, as opposed to the cost of goods sold that directly relate to the products or services for sale. Your overhead is what you have to pay every month that doesn't make you money. These are the things you have to pay to stay in business, but you can make sure you are not paying more than you need to, therefore creating more profit. You can decide for yourself what you want to pay for these things. Maybe you can work out of a smaller, cheaper office space, or maybe you want a large office space. You can work with these bills to create what you want at the price you want and can afford. I purchased as

much used office furniture as I could. I saved thousands of dollars doing this. I also learned marketing to save money on advertising. You have to decide how you want your business to be perceived and what you are comfortable with. Maybe you could share an office or work from a home office to start out.

MANAGING PAYABLES

Accounts payable are the unpaid bills of your business; the money you owe to your suppliers and other creditors. If you have an invoice in front of you with terms of payment, you probably had to fill out a credit application to get that credit extended to you. If you can get a discount for paying early, do it. If not, pay when the bill is due, but don't be late and incur a late fee. You can sometimes even renegotiate your payment terms if you have been a good payer in the past or purchase a lot each month. You can ask your vendor or supplier to offer you a pre-payment discount. It is worth a try to ask—all they can say is no, or they can say yes, and you can be that much richer each time you pay.

When setting up your accounts with your suppliers, negotiate the best payment terms you can and try to include an early pay discount. Always check the invoices you receive and make sure there aren't any hidden fees or overcharges, such as shipping, insurance, sales tax, or anything else you did not agree to. Make sure you are charged the amount you agreed upon. For example, if something was on sale or you purchased in bulk to save money, make sure you were not billed erroneously at the original price. Mistakes happen and it is your responsibility to check your invoices for any errors. They may seem like small errors, but when they happen throughout the year, it can add up. If you do find an error, call the vendor or supplier right away and ask for a corrected invoice to be faxed to you immediately.

SEEKING UP-FRONT PAYMENTS

Sometimes a customer will want to make a large purchase or need some work done that is beyond their budget. Even if they are a credit-approved customer, you should always try to get half of the payment up front, and maybe let them charge the balance or get the balance at the time of completion. Most customers making a large purchase will gladly pay the partial payment up front, but not if you don't ask. This has been my experience, and it is much harder to get paid the full amount afterward. Make it a policy or rule and you can blame the policy manual. Whenever this situation arises, let them know you require half the money up front with the balance due upon completion of the job, shipment, order, or whatever it might be. You can have special agreements in your word processor all ready to be printed out and signed for this customer's file. It is like a special credit agreement for this one large purchase.

EVALUATE YOUR PRICING

Along with being too easy on extending credit, start-up entrepreneurs are often unrealistic about the prices they charge and normally they end up charging too little. Make sure you know how much something will cost you to deliver before quoting a price. If you are doing service work, and think a job may take two hours and it ends

up taking five, you have lost money. Do not promise more than you can do. Be realistic and try to do more than you say you will. I have sometimes told clients a job would take me a week when I knew it would take three to four days, because I wanted to be able to deliver early if I could. This is great customer service.

To evaluate your pricing, see what others in your field are charging. What does that include? Remember, cheaper is not always better. You get what you pay for. So don't think you have to come up with the cheapest price to make your pricing work for you. People will pay more for good quality work or products. Gather as much information as you can on what the competition offers and what is included in that price. See if you can come close, based on what you will be paying your suppliers and on your overhead. Try to negotiate on something like shipping to be able to lower your price. You also could offer discounts on bulk purchases or when someone pays up front.

RUNNING A PROFITABLE, DEBT-FREE, SMALL BUSINESS

As you can see you can run a profitable, debt-free business. You can start a business from your home, having little overhead, or maybe get a small business loan and open an office or store front. Either way, you can end up debt-free and making a profit. You might end up getting a small office space and paying off your loan early because you created a credit policy and everyone always pays you on time. If you are smart and plan ahead when starting your business, you can make this work. Having the three plans in place—business plan, credit and collections plan, and marketing plan—will help this happen for you. No matter what happens, you have your plans to fall back on.

Try to purchase your office supplies from a bulk wholesaler such as a warehouse rather than an office supply store, which can be expensive. Try to purchase your supplies from vendors who are local and you can save on shipping costs. Attend your chamber meetings and try to barter with other business owners—this is a great way to network and support other business owners in your area and save money. Don't wait until you're in a bind or your business is in trouble before cutting costs or looking at your financial picture—it will be too late. Make it a point to look at your finances throughout the year or at least once a year so you can make any changes that may make the coming year more profitable. Don't get so caught up in the day-to-day running of your store or office that you lose sight of running your business. Schedule time, even if it is just once a month, to really look at your business and how it is doing. Doing this once a week is better, but if you feel like you can't do that, at least do it once a month, maybe when you are paying your bills.

FOCUS ON SALES AND REDUCE EXPENSES

It is true that if you want to improve profits, you must reduce expenses and/or make more sales. Making expense improvements requires internal actions as well as working with customers and suppliers. If you can reduce expenses and still maintain at least the same level of sales, your profits should increase. One of the ways you can do this is with marketing. You should be market-ing all the time for the life of your business. If you cut back on marketing, your sales and profits will suffer. One of the easiest and most profitable ways to make more sales and reduce expenses is to market to your existing clients. It is much easier to make another sale to an existing customer than to obtain a new one. You can do this by offering a special deal, such as free shipping; buy one, get one free; or a discount on the purchase of item #2. For example, buy one of my books at full price and get the second at 50 percent off. You also can contact existing customers and offer them a discount or free gift if they refer someone to you.

If you focus on your sales, remember that the more attention you give a customer, the less price matters. Customers will pay more for quality customer service. Make sure you are helping your customers and giving them the time they deserve. Without them, you wouldn't have a business. Ask them if they know of anyone else who might be interested in your services—if they are happy, they may refer someone to you. You never know who that might be—it could be the biggest customer you ever obtain! Always ask questions. Ask your customers if they are happy with your services or product. Ask them if there is anything you could improve. Give your customers a product and service questionnaire to complete. Customer service is a continual activity—make sure you don't put it on the back burner or you will lose customers.

ADVANTAGES OF PROMPT INVOICING FOR ANY SMALL BUSINESS OWNER

I know I have already covered this but it is so important to your cash flow that I want to reiterate on this point: One of the easiest and cheapest ways to keep your cash flow flowing smoothly is to invoice customers immediately after the transaction is complete. There is no reason to wait. Once you send the invoice, your 30 days (if those are your terms) has started. The longer you wait, the longer the customer has to pay. You want your money right away or as soon as possible. If you only do one thing, do this. It will help increase your cash flow immensely. So many business owners set up their billing to be done once a month or twice a month. I don't understand this reasoning if they want to get paid quickly.

In order to keep track of the money flowing in and out of your business you need to follow these steps:

- Measure your cash flow: Try to project cash flow by looking at your bills and watching if they go up or down. You cannot predict your future but you can make an educated guess at how things might go. Part of your cash flow will be the bad debt you recover, the sales you make, and interest earnings. You also have to have a good idea of how much cash you spend each week or month. You need to make these projections if you want to have a successful future.

- Improve your accounts receivables: You can do this by speeding up the payment process. Some of the ways you can do this are to offer early payment discounts to your customers—on large jobs get half of the money up front, have a credit policy and check people's credit, sell off old inventory that is sitting around your business, have a sale to move it quickly. Bill your customers immediately after providing your service or delivering your product. Keep your eye on slow-paying customers and revoke the credit of anyone who gets past due or gives you a bad check.

CHAPTER 16

Collection Downfalls of New and Small Business Owners

THERE ARE SOME COMMON MISTAKES for all new or small business owners. When people start a new business they are not familiar with these things and tend to make the same mistakes that have been made before them. Because you have purchased this book, I know you don't want to make those same mistakes.

There are always some companies that have past due invoices and can't seem to get them paid. They might be quietly waiting to get paid not wanting to contact the client for fear of appearing "desperate." Sometimes a big part of the problem is no response—it is bad enough when you are not getting paid, but when orders keep coming in and you are not getting any acknowledgment to your collection efforts you just can't keep processing orders.

There are steps you can take to get paid on those past due invoices and keep new invoices current.

Step 1. Gather together all the past due invoices for each customer, and stamp them PAST DUE. Use red, blue, or green ink.

Step 2. If you have an e-mail address or phone number with a contact name for your client, e-mail them or call them and give them the information on the past due invoices and let them know their account is on hold.

Step 3. Mail the invoices to your customer with return receipt requested or send them in a flat rate priority mail envelope with delivery confirmation.

Step 4. Send a letter with these invoices stating the age, invoice numbers, their purchase order numbers, your account number, total amount due, and any other pertinent information.

Step 5. Tell them their account is on hold and you will not be shipping any more products or providing any services to them until these invoices are paid. You can include a self-addressed envelope and state that you have enclosed an envelope for them to send their check. Give them a due date to have this paid to you.

Once they have received the package, e-mail or call them. Ask them what they are doing with the invoices. Ask them questions such as: Do these invoices have to be approved by someone else? If they have to be approved, who has to approve them and when will they give them to that person? Get that person's direct number if possible. Find out if that person signs the checks. Are there any discrepancies with the invoices? When will the check be cut? When can you call back for the check number?

Once all the past due balances are cleared up, you need to think about future invoices. Do you want to extend credit again or do you want to have pre-payment or payment at the time of the order? Whatever you decide, put it in writing. If you can both sign the agreement, that is even better. Remember, having a credit policy in place tells people you mean business.

GETTING NEW CUSTOMER INFORMATION

One of the most important things you can do when you open your doors is to collect information on any new customer. So many new business owners are so excited to make a sale or have some

interest in their product that they skip this step. Use the sample credit application in this book, or in any of my other books, or purchase some at an office supply store. This is such an easy step to take and can save you so much time, money, effort, and frustration that it is almost silly not to do it. You can get more detailed or involved in what information you request or just have a simple, basic generic form for every new potential customer to fill out. Once you make this mandatory, there should not be a client without one on file. If you find there is a customer file without a completed credit application, have them fill one out. You should have a signed credit application for every customer you have. Never ship products or provide a service to someone whom you do not have any information on.

CHECKING CUSTOMER INFORMATION AND CREATING ACCOUNTS

Once you have the credit application, *check the information* before creating an account. You may decide you do not want this person as a customer or maybe you won't want to extend credit. Some business owners get a credit application but do not check the references or credit of the customer. They claim that it is a waste of time, because everyone puts good references anyway—why would they list a bad reference? They also believe that having the filled-out form is enough because if the person doesn't pay, they will be placing the account with an outside collection agency and they will use the information on the form to collect for them.

This is true; when you place an account with an outside collection agency, if you can provide them with a completed, signed credit application, they have a better chance of collecting for you. If you are not interested in doing inhouse collections, this might be the route for you. You need to decide how much you want to handle inhouse and how much time, energy, and money you want to invest in creating and enforcing a credit policy.

GETTING PAID

If you take the steps outlined in this book, you should have more accounts that pay than not. There will always be customers who start out paying great, then start slacking or paying slower as time goes on. If they see they can get away with paying in 45 or 55 days rather than 30 without any reaction from you, they will. You need to stay on top of your accounts for the duration of their business with you. When you enforce a credit policy and demand to get paid for your work, you will not alienate good customers. If a customer is annoyed or upset that you are trying to get paid or enforce your credit policy, you probably don't want them as a customer anyway. So let them go to the competition. This way you end up with all the good paying customers, have a steady cash flow, make more money, and can be successful. The competition will end up with all the slow or nonpaying customers and will not grow or be as successful as you will. If you present yourself and your business in a professional manner, word will get around and you will be respected and rewarded for your good business sense.

Finally, the checklist of items that you need to do before making the sale follows:

- Get a signed credit application
- Check the customer's information and/or credit

- Make the sale on your terms
- Get paid

RESOURCES

I have tried to include many resources that will help you create and maintain the ultimate credit policy for your business. I am listing them here for you so you can use them easily. If you come across any other resources that I might have missed that you feel would be helpful, please e-mail them to me at michelle@michelledunn.com so I may include them in future editions.

Equifax
P.O. Box 740241
Atlanta, GA 30374-0241
800-685-1111
www.equifax.com

Experian
P.O. Box 2002
Allen, TX 75013
888-397-3742
www.experian.com

TransUnion
P.O. Box 1000
Chester, PA 19022
800-916-8800
www.transunion.com

www.michelledunn.com. To order books that include debt collection letters, laws, and forms to help you in the creation and enforcement of your credit policy.

www.credit-and-collections.com. To join a free online networking group where you can ask over 800 members anything related to credit, debt collection, and credit policies. Also browse the articles and free e-books available on the site to aid you in enforcing your credit policy. Read the Fair Debt Collection Practices Act and more laws, tips, and resources to help you.

www.checkman.com. Download software and purchase special check paper to process and print checks inhouse.

https://www.thawte.com. Create a secure web page where customers and clients can securely pay you online with credit cards, checks, debit cards, or online payment options.

www.ftc.gov. The Federal Trade Commission official web site with all the laws and updates you need to follow when creating and enforcing your credit policy.

www.lawdog.com/state/laws.htm. State laws about debt collection listed by state, easy to use.

www.inc.com/guides/growth/23032.html. Full of business information and tips to help you with your communication skills.

www.mediate.com. Helpful information and tips on learning mediation.

www.shopgetorganized.com. Organize your thoughts and your office.

www.viking.com. Office supplies and forms.

www.officemax.com. Even more office supplies!

www.challengebp.com. Check out this site for printed envelopes, to include with dunning letters.

www.rentons.com. The best past due stickers I have ever seen. I have used this company for years.

www.homebusinessmag.com. *Home Business Magazine*, full of helpful tips and resources to help you start, run, and expand your business.

www.entrepreneur.com. You can subscribe to their popular magazine and order books like this one to help you in your business with marketing, growing, business plans, and so much more.

www.morebusiness.com. This web site offers sample business plans, contracts, and information on marketing.

www.irs.gov. The Internal Revenue Service official web site has checklists for businesses, information on employees, deductions and credits, record-keeping and accounting methods. It also includes many tax topics and frequently asked questions.

www.businessinfoguide.com. This is a great site that has information, articles, tools, and resources for entrepreneurs.

www.msfinancialsavvy.com. Another great site that is geared toward women, but all are welcome! Learn about small business, investing, saving money, and much more.

www.sba.gov. The official site of the United States Small Business Association will give you the tools to learn about business development, financing, research, and more.

www.mybusinessmag.com. This magazine has over 60,000 subscribers and can give you tools and tips to help you in every aspect of your business.

www.inc.com. This site has articles, tips, and a free daily e-mail of top news stories so you can keep up to date in your industry.

www.startupjournal.com. This *Wall Street Journal* center includes articles, tools, a bookstore, chat rooms, and free networking.

www.trpaulsen.com. My friend Tim runs this site and it is all about training, products, free tips, and tools to help you collect more money.

www.creditadvisers.info. This is a great site run by Darryl Douglas, which offers credit reports and other decision-making data and services.

www.eliresearch.com. This newsletter is something you will want to subscribe to and keep up to date on trends in the debt collection industry as well as on what is happening in your industry.

Credit and Collection Letters

THIS APPENDIX PROVIDES YOU WITH LETTERS that correspond to different chapters in the book that you can use to resolve various credit and collections situations and claims. These also are included on the CD that accompanies this book. Of course you can modify them as appropriate to your needs and circumstances.

DISPUTE LETTER—CHAPTER 1

Date
Your Name
Your Address
Your City, State ZIP

Complaint Department
Name of Credit Reporting Agency
Address
City, State ZIP

Dear Sir or Madam:

I am writing to dispute the following information in my file. The items I dispute are also encircled on the attached copy of the report I received. (Identify the item(s) disputed by name, and identify the type of item, such as credit account, judgment, etc.)

This item is (inaccurate or incomplete) because (describe what is inaccurate or incomplete and why). I am requesting that the item be deleted (or request another specific change) to correct the information.

Enclosed are copies of (use this sentence if applicable and describe any enclosed documentation, such as payment records or court documents) supporting my position. Please reinvestigate this (these) matter(s) and (delete or correct) the disputed item(s) as soon as possible.

Sincerely,

Name
Title

AUTOMATIC BILL PAY AUTHORIZATION FORM FOR CHECKS/CHECKING ACCOUNTS—CHAPTER 4

Your Company Name

Date
Your customer's name and address

Dear

By signing and returning this form, you are giving permission to YOUR COMPANY NAME to print one or more drafts as listed below to be drawn against the following account(s):

Bank name   Bank transit numbers   Check number

Such drafts will be used as payments towards your account(s) listed with YOUR COMPANY NAME.

Your current balance of all accounts listed is $100.00.

Please sign and date this form and return to:

COMPANY NAME AND ADDRESS

Draft date   Draft number   Draft amount

Signature _____Date_____

Remember to void these checks in your checkbook, and enter the amounts and dates into your check register.

Sincerely,

Your company name
Your name
Your title

CREDIT CARD AUTHORIZATION FORM–CHAPTER 4

Date _____

Account # _____

Company name _____

Address _____

Phone _____

Cardholders Name _____

Type of Card: ❏ MasterCard   ❏ VISA   ❏ AMEX   ❏ Discover

Card number _____

Expiration Date _____

I hereby authorize (your company name) to automatically charge the above credit card whenever I place an order with them, unless there is a prior written notice.

Signature of cardholder _____

Date _____

REQUEST FOR CREDIT REFERENCES—CHAPTER 5

Name _____

Date _____

Mailing Address _____

Legal Business Name (if applicable) _____

Phone _____ Fax _____ E-mail _____

Manner of payment _____

Discounts _____

Prompt ❏   Slow ❏

How many days _____

C.O.D. Account _____

Customer since _____

High credit $_____   Amount now owing $_____

Past due amount $_____   Terms _____

Comments
_____

Banks _____

Name _____

Address _____

Phone _____ Fax _____ E-mail _____

Average Checking Account Balance $_____

NSF Checks $_____

Loan Experiences _____

Customer Since _____

Security Held _____

Comments _____

PROSPECTIVE APPLICANT DENIAL LETTER–CHAPTER 5

Date

Dear

Your application for credit with YOUR COMPANY NAME has unfortunately been denied.

One or more of the reasons for the denial of your application may be found below:

❏ Information contained in a consumer credit report was obtained from: (See List Below)
❏ A consumer credit report containing information insufficient to our need was obtained from: (See List Below)
❏ The fact that the consumer reporting agency contacted was unable to supply any information about you. (See List)
❏ Information was received from a person or company other than a consumer reporting agency. You have a right to make a written request within 60 days of receiving this letter for a disclosure of the nature of this information.

Pursuant to federal law, we are prohibited from disclosing the source of this information.

When a credit report is used in making the decision, the Fair Credit Reporting act requires us to tell you where we obtained that report.

That company may also have obtained information on you from one or more of the consumer reporting agencies whose names, addresses and phone numbers are listed below. They and the other agencies only provide information about your credit history. They took no part in making the decision, nor can they explain why this decision was made. The following (checked) consumer reporting agencies supplied your credit information:

❏ Experian (TRW) Consumer Assistance, P.O. Box 949, Allen, TX 75002 800-682-7654
❏ Trans Union Consumer Relations, P.O. Box 1000, 2 Baldwin Place, Chester, PA 19022 800-888-4213
❏ CBI/Equifax Credit Information Services, P.O. Box 740241, Atlanta, GA 30374-2041 800-685-1111

You have certain rights under federal law to get a copy of your report, dispute its accuracy and insert a consumer statement. If you believe your file contains errors, is inaccurate or incomplete call the consumer reporting agency that has been checked at their toll-free number, or write to them using the information listed above for disclosure. The disclosure can be made orally, in writing or electronically. You also have a right during the 60 day period that starts DATE to receive a free copy of your consumer report from the consumer reporting agency whose name is checked off above.

You have a right to dispute the accuracy or completeness of any information contained in your consumer credit report, as furnished by the consumer reporting agency whose name is checked off above. You have the right to put into your file a consumer statement up to 100 words in length to explain items in your file.

Customer assistance at the credit reporting agency whose name has been checked is available to help you with the consumer statement.

You may have additional rights under the credit reporting or consumer protection laws of your state. If you wish you may contact your state or local consumer protection agency or a state Attorney General's office.

Thank you for your application. I wish you the best in your future endeavors.

Sincerely,

Name
Title

CREDIT APPROVED LETTER–CHAPTER 5

Date

Name and Address

Dear

Thank you for applying for credit with YOUR COMPANY NAME. We are happy to tell you that your account has been approved and your credit limit is $5000.00.

Please refer to the back of this notice for our terms and conditions for payment.

Sincerely,

Name
Title

FRIENDLY REMINDER LETTER—CHAPTER 8

Date

Name and address

Dear

Please be advised that your account has a past due balance of $100 that was due on Date. Please send your payment of $100 today in the enclosed payment envelope to bring your account current.

Please call this office at (phone number) if there is a reason you have not paid this balance. Thank you for your prompt attention to this important matter.

Sincerely,

Name
Title

SECOND NOTICE–CHAPTER 8

Date

Name and address

Dear

We sent you a first notice on Date, requesting your payment of $100 to clear up the past due balance on your account. To date we have not had a response or received your payment.

Your payment, or any questions you may have, should be directed to this office to ensure proper credit to your account. You may also pay online at (web site address) for your payment to be immediately credited to your account.

Sincerely,

Name
Title

FINAL NOTICE—CHAPTER 8

Date

Name and address

Dear

Because you have failed to respond to our previous letters, this is an attempt at an amicable resolution of your account.

Unless your remittance reaches our office within the next seven (7) days, we will be forced to take further action. We urge you to send your payment today or call to pay by credit card or with a check by phone. You can also pay online at (web site address) or call toll free 1-800 (number) or write us at (business mailing address).

We would like to resolve this matter and put it behind us as much as you do. But we are committed to taking whatever steps are necessary and proper to enforce payment of your obligation.

Sincerely,

Name
Title

CONFIRMATION OF A PAYMENT PROMISE LETTER—CHAPTER 8

Date

Name and address

Dear

This letter is to confirm the commitment you made in our telephone conversation. You stated that a check would be mailed on DATE in the amount of $100.00.

Thank you in advance for your payment.

Sincerely,

Name
Title

CONFIRMATION OF A PAYMENT PLAN LETTER—CHAPTER 8

Date

Name and address

Dear

This letter is to confirm the commitment you made on the phone today. As agreed, you will send $25 a week starting Friday, November 4, 2007 by postal mail in the form of a check to (your business address) You will then send $25 every Friday until the balance is paid in full. Until this balance is paid all new orders will be on a pre-paid basis.

Enclosed please find a payment envelope for your first payment.

Sincerely,

Name
Title

Sample Credit Application

Firm Name: _____ Contact person: _____

Address: _____

City: _____ State: _____ Zip: _____

Type of business: _____ Year business opened: _____

Phone: _____ Fax: _____ Email: _____

Federal ID# or SS# : _____ Principals name: _____

Bank Reference

Name: _____ Account #: _____

Address: _____

City: _____ State: _____ Zip: _____

Phone: _____ Date account opened: _____

Trade References

Firm name: _____ Phone: _____

Firm name: _____ Phone: _____

Firm name: _____ Phone: _____

The undersigned hereby agrees that, should a credit account be opened, and in the event of default in the payment of any amount due, and if such account is submitted to a collection authority, to pay an additional charge equal to the cost of collection including court costs.

Company: _____ Date: _____

Signature: _____ Title: _____

Please print your name: _____

CHECK RETURNED LETTER

Date

Debtor name
Address
City, State ZIP

Dear Debtor:

Your check # _____ in the amount of $_____ was returned to us as "Account Closed."

Perhaps you closed the account not realizing this check was outstanding?

Please send a new check for $_____ to replace it today.

Sincerely,

Name
Title

DEDUCTIONS LETTER

Date:

Debtor name
Debtor address
Debtor city, state ZIP

Account number:

Balance due:

Dear debtor:

Thank you for your letter of (date) and your check in the amount of $_____.

After careful review of the deductions you have taken, we feel that the following Disputed amounts are invalid:

Labor Services	$290.00
Mileage	$109.80
Potential Equipment Defects	$250.00
Total Deductions:	$649.80

To help us resolve this matter as quickly as possible, please provide documentation to support the deductions you have taken.

If you have any questions, please call us anytime at (PHONE).

Thank you for your help in resolving this matter.

Sincerely,

Name
Title

SAMPLE ENVELOPE ENCLOSED LETTER

Date

Debtor name
Address
City, State ZIP

Account #:

Balance Due $_____

Dear Debtor:

After reviewing our accounts, we find that your balance of $_____ is more than 30 days overdue. As you know, payment is due upon receipt of the invoice.

Call us if you have any questions regarding your account balance at (PHONE).

Please send your payment upon receipt of this letter. We have enclosed an envelope for your convenience.

Sincerely,

Name
Address

NSF CHECKS LETTER

Date

Debtor name
Address
City, State ZIP

Dear Debtor:

Your check dated (month, day, year), was returned to us for "insufficient funds."

We will redeposit this check on (month, day, year). Please make sure there are sufficient funds to cover this check in the amount of $_____.

Sincerely,

Name
Title

PARTIAL PAYMENTS LETTER

Date

Debtor name
Address
City, State ZIP

Dear Debtor:

Thank you for your payment of $_____ towards your balance. The balance due of $_____ remains past due.

Please mail your check for $_____ today.

A postpaid envelope is enclosed for your payment.

Sincerely,

Name
Title

PAYMENT REMINDER LETTER

Date

Debtor name
Address
City, State ZIP

Dear Debtor:

Account #

Dear Debtor:

This is just a reminder that your payment of $_____has not been received in our office. If you forgot to mail us your payment, please send it today. If you have already mailed your check, please disregard this reminder.

Thank you,

Name
Title

PLACING FOR COLLECTION LETTER

Date

Debtor name
Address
City, State ZIP

Account #:

Balance Due $_____

Dear Debtor:

The services of (company name) were provided to you with the expectation that you would pay for them.

Your check needs to be received in our office within 48 hours of your receipt of this letter or we will place your account with an outside collection agency.

Sincerely,

Name
Title

RETURN CALL LETTER

Date

Debtor name
Address
City, State ZIP

Account #:

Dear Debtor:

Ignoring your obligations does not make them go away. This is especially true with seriously past due debts.

Late fees and interest can cause your balance to increase, and without your response, there is nothing we can do to stop this.

We are willing to work with you and would appreciate the courtesy of a return call.

Sincerely,

Name
Title

SMALL AMOUNTS #1

Date

Debtor name
Address
City, State ZIP

Dear Debtor:

Your check for $_____ has not been received. This may be a small amount, but all overdue amounts are meaningful to us.

Please mail your check for $_____ today.

Sincerely,

Name
Title

SMALL AMOUNTS #2

Date

Debtor name
Address
City, State ZIP

Dear Debtor:

It may seem a nuisance for us to remind you of your past due balance of $_____$, and it may seem a bother for you to pay such a small amount immediately.

However, payment of this small balance would be very much appreciated.

Sincerely,

Name
Title

THE 3-LETTER SERIES
Letter #1

Date

Debtor name
Address
City, State ZIP

Account #:

Account balance $_____

Dear Debtor:

Here is a reminder that your account of $ _____ was overdue as of (date). Please pay this account promptly. If you have already put the check in the mail, we apologize for the inconvenience and thank you for your payment.

Sincerely,

THE 3-LETTER SERIES
Letter #2

Date

Debtor name
Address
City, State ZIP

Account #:

Account balance $_____

Dear Debtor:

This is the second reminder that you owe us $_____. Please pay this account promptly. We would like to continue doing business with you, but we need your cooperation and payment to do so.

Thank you for your prompt attention to this matter.

Sincerely,

Name
Title

THE 3-LETTER SERIES
Letter #3

Date

Debtor name
Address
City, State ZIP

Account #:

Account balance $_____

Dear Debtor:

This is your final reminder that your account balance of $_____ is past due. It has been past due since _____, _____. If payment is not received by (date), we will have no alternative but to turn your account over to a (lawyer or collection agency) for collection.

Thank you for your prompt attention to this matter.

Sincerely,

Name
Title

How to Turn Prospects into Credit-Approved Customers

STILL NOT SURE IF YOU NEED A CREDIT policy? In my opinion, every business needs one but let me share some more information with you that can help you make a decision that will benefit you, your business, your employees and your customers.

There are powerful strategies that business owners can use to dramatically improve their sales, income, and bottom line.

With this book in hand, business owners can hone their credit polices and maximize the number of prospects they turn into credit-approved customers immediately.

The first strategy is to increase awareness within your organization about your credit policy. Have a written credit policy and make sure everyone abides by it; if just one department or person doesn't it can all fall apart. Keep your eye on the sales department; they will come to the credit manager the most often with requests for leniency.

A second strategy is having one person in charge of all credit applications and new account information. All of the information obtained is extremely confidential. One person should be handling the processing of all the new account forms and credit applications and reports and keeping them in a locked file cabinet. Some business owners have a credit manager who would be in charge of all the credit information.

Speed is another issue that is important. Consumers today are looking for fast, easy answers. The more streamlined your credit policy is, the happier your prospects will be. If it's easy and it's fast, your customer will be happy and spread the word.

HOW IMPORTANT IS A CREDIT POLICY AND WHY DO I NEED ONE?

"Know your customers." Every business owner knows how important it is to keep your customers happy and coming back for more.

A credit policy is relevant to every business's customers. If you don't know your customers and don't make your policy and forms easy, fast, and simple to understand, you could lose the customer, taking the sale with them and any word of mouth advertising.

So what can business owners do to make their credit policy effective? First, business owners should implement a credit procedure for any new or existing customers. They should learn exactly what customers are looking for when they apply for credit with their company.

Business owners should place new customer packets or credit applications on their reception desk in a highly visible place, with clipboards and pens. When a potential customer walks in they can fill this out quickly and easily and be on their way to having a new credit-approved charge account.

Catering to a potential new customer is good business anyway, so the easier you make it for them to spend more money with you, the more money and more sales will benefit you and your business.

HOW TO WRITE A CREDIT POLICY FOR YOUR BUSINESS

The different ways people use and extend credit makes or breaks your credit policy and bottom line, which could result in less or more sales and money for your business.

Business owners all have different types of businesses but can all extend credit, so it should only make sense that no two credit polices can be the same.

One major difference is if you have a service or retail business. Your credit policy should use multiple facets to cater to prospective customers but also protect the business owner.

You are limited in what you can and can't ask a prospective customer in order to extend them credit. All business owners need to be aware of what these questions are and what the laws are before they create their credit policy. Your credit policy helps to filter customers so you don't have to spend your time chasing your money. Your best policy will be short, easy, and to the point, and it will avoid long-winded statements and a lot of legal or big words. Always create your forms with the reader in mind, the easier and clearer the better.

How customer friendly is your credit policy?

It's a classic mistake for business owners. They start a business that is focused on their product and not on the credit end of their business.

Your goal is to have more customers who pay on time, which translates to higher or more sales.

You have a lot of different people with a lot of different needs, depending on your business; the first step is a customer-friendly credit policy that ensures you have the information you need if there is ever a payment problem, but also one that doesn't scare away your customers.

It is important that you maintain customer relations but also protect yourself and your business from bad debt, bad checks, or slow or non-paying customers.

The second step is to have the policy in effect before obtaining the new customer and making sure everyone in your organization is familiar with it and enforces it. It is not very professional to search for a credit application or not know which forms they have to fill out to open a new account.

If you find your credit application is not working for you or you are having problems with some aspect of your credit policy, you can change it at any time and measure your results to be sure they are working for you.

The best strategy for making your credit policy work is to look at your bottom line and also ask your customers if they had any problems with the forms or the information they had to provide, and keep asking.

How can you tell if your credit policy is working?

If you don't have a credit policy, everyone will want to buy from you. This can result in unpaid and past due invoices on your books.

Customers and business owners can tell if you are professional or on top of your game just by your policies. If you extend credit without getting a credit application filled out, customers know you aren't serious and this could lead to payment issues down the road.

If you have a credit policy and have every new customer fill out a credit application, some will run away as fast as they can, and others will happily fill them out. One goal accomplished. You can use parts or all of the suggestions in this book to create steady cash flow by streamlining your accounts receivable and credit departments.

HOW TO GIVE YOUR CUSTOMERS A CHOICE BETWEEN YOU AND THE COMPETITION AND HAVE THEM CHOOSE YOU

Instead of giving your customers or potential customers a choice between you and your competition and having them choose the other guy, have them choose you.

Some customers, when given the choice between signing a credit application and paying at the time of sale, mostly choose the credit application regardless of who has the cheaper prices. It is true that some customers will buy more from you if they are approved for credit and have more time to pay. It makes it easy for them to place orders and receive a bill, rather than have to pay at the point of sale.

Like everything else, the easier you make it for the customer to buy from you the more sales you will have. Customers want things to be easy, fast, and instant. If they are credit approved and can call and order and have the item quickly, then pay when they receive a bill, they will be more likely to order from you than someone who doesn't offer that option, resulting in your business making more money and more sales.

ARE YOU SCARING AWAY POTENTIAL CUSTOMERS?

When you are trying to make a sale and ask someone to fill out a credit application and new account form, do your potential customers turn around and run to the competition?

You can avoid scaring customers away and keep them coming back. First, find out what your competition is doing; do they have a credit policy? If they do, what is included? What does their credit application look like? How many forms do new customers have to fill out? Do they have good paying customers? Look online; a lot of business web site will have their credit applications available online.

It is amazing how much "stuff" people will jam onto their credit applications and new account forms. This alone can scare a potential customer away, especially if they can go down the road and fill out one easy form and have their product or service.

Consumers get distracted by long forms, especially ones that ask for too much information or are full of legal jargon or long technical terms. Keep your form short and to the point. Keep the language easy to understand and in everyday terms.

Don't sweat the small stuff with your credit policy – it's not as scary as it seems!

Do you know how many customers you have that are past due right now? How many bad checks are sitting on your desk that you don't know what to do with? How many dunning letters do you send out a month?

How would you like to answer those questions with none, or very few? One thing that is often overlooked is how to prevent future credit issues. I am always amazed at how creditors will hire someone to collect the bad debt they have but do nothing to prevent future problems.

Business owners should implement a credit policy before they start their business; it should be included in their business plan. If you're an existing business with bad debt, you can create a credit policy and implement it with existing and future customers right now.

If you have a pile of bad debt, it is never too late to implement a credit policy. The sooner you do it, the better your chances are of collecting what is already owed to you and preventing future bad debt, so you won't be in this situation again.

HOW BUSINESSES MESS UP THEIR CREDIT POLICIES

One mistake business owners make is not having a credit policy in place when they open their business. This can be easily corrected by implementing one at any time. At the very least, every business should have every customer fill out a credit application.

In the business's view, it seems easier to just process the order without obtaining any or limited information on the customer. Most new business are so excited to make the sale they don't want to offend the customer by asking them to fill out a credit application.

Another mistake business owners make is not to ask for the money once it is due. They were so happy to make the sale, and now don't want to make the customer mad by asking for the money, even if it is past due. This is your money, do not work for free!

Show potential customers that you are proud of what you do and that you are serious, and have a sound credit policy in place. The customer that is offended or doesn't want to fill out the credit application is probably not someone you want as a customer anyway.

HOW BUSINESSES CAN STOP WALLOWING IN BAD DEBT AND PREVENT IT IN THE FUTURE

One of the best things you can do is to implement a credit policy or have each new customer fill out a credit application. This cannot be said enough. A credit application will protect you and let your customers know you mean business. Done correctly, it can increase your overall profits now and in the future.

Having a sound credit policy in place helps ensure that you will get paid, as long as it is enforced. Most customers who open accounts for credit expect to fill out something and will not complain, but will realize you are serious and smart about your business.

Customers who have to fill out forms when they set up an account might also take advantage of direct pay options, which lowers your receivables immediately and creates more sales for your business.

It may cost you some money to have credit applications and other forms printed, and hire someone to run your Credit Department or do credit checks, but it will result in more money for you and your business.

HOW TO MAKE MORE MONEY EXTENDING CREDIT

Easy, quick and painless. If your credit policy is flowing smoothly, it is probably all of these.

Some steps you can take to make your credit policy easy, quick and painless are:

1. Make it easy for the customer to get credit with you. Have packets paper-clipped together at the front desk; include the credit application, automatic payment permission forms, and anything else you want filled out before opening an account.
2. Make it quick, by having these packets ready and waiting for anyone who comes in. Have pens and clip boards available so they can be filled out immediately.
3. Make it painless, by either having them wait and running the credit application while they are still there or responding to them within a certain time period, say 24 hours.

Consumers today, like everyone else, are expecting convenience and speed. If you make opening up a credit account difficult or are unorganized, you might lose the customer.

Customers that are approved for credit will buy more if they can pay later, so make the process as streamlined as you can.

Tips to Help You Make More Money and More Sales with a Credit Policy

SOME BUSINESS OWNERS ASK WHY DO I need a credit policy? I don't have much bad debt. The following will help you understand and decide if you want or need to implement a credit policy. It is my belief that every business should have a credit policy.

The objective of a sound credit policy should be:

- To provide timely notification to customers regarding past due amounts, therefore eliminating old balances from being carried on the receivables.
- To outline a procedure that will provide customers with options when they cannot pay in full and on time.
- To provide a procedure on when and what to do with small balances on customers' accounts.

- To provide a procedure that will enable a company to adequately provide reasonable credit limits for customers with revolving credit.
- To provide guidelines to legally collect money due your company that was lost because of bad checks.
- To have a system that will maintain timely contact with customers when they are past due.
- To provide a procedure that will enable your company to keep credit card numbers on file for customers and automatically charge them when they place an order.
- To have a procedure that will enable your company to be aware of when an account should be placed for collection and to avoid carrying bad debts on the receivables.

- To provide a procedure that will enable your business to legally charge customers' credit cards at the time they place an order.
- To provide a procedure that will eliminate orders being held, and to better serve customers in a timely manner.
- To have a procedure that will enable your business to be aware of when to write a balance off to bad debt.

Small business owners sometimes make some common mistakes when just starting out, and trying to get paid. Some small business owners depend on that income more than someone who gets a check each week. This is because when you work for yourself, the work and therefore the payments are sporadic.

Small business owners just starting out are sometimes so eager to make a sale that they will accept work or an order without getting a signed contract or checking credit references. They just wait and wait to be paid because they don't want to offend the customer or appear that they NEED the money. This happens more often than not. ALWAYS have a written contract or agreement. You may also want to get half of the money up front with terms regarding the balance very specifically addressed in your agreement. If you can get the other party to sign the agreement, that is even better.

It is worth it to try and collect the money due at first. Make a couple of calls, but if promises are made but no payment, think about using a collection service. It shows you are serious and don't work for free. Word will get around that you mean business. Your customers will know you are serious if:

- They have to fill out a Credit Application
- They have to sign a contract
- They receive invoices right away
- You *send* your invoices right away, as soon as items have shipped or the work is complete
- You call right away if you don't receive payment. Don't wait!
- You gather all the information you can about the debtor
- You are professional at all times
- You are persistent
- You make personal visits when you can
- You offer different payment methods
- You charge a late fee and/or finance charge

Extending credit works in your favor in many ways. It increases customer loyalty. Taking a financial risk for your customers demonstrates you trust them and are willing to accommodate them. If you extend credit be sure you have a credit policy in effect. A credit policy also indicates your business is financially stable. A business in danger of going under does not give its customers the option of paying at a later date. A struggling business demands payments immediately. Be sure to mark your terms clearly on any invoices and statements you send out.

Credit policies increase sales for another reason. Some customers are unable to pay for a product or service in its entirety. If customers have the option to pay for items in monthly installments, they will be more inclined to make purchases that do not fall within their current budgets.

Extending credit also has downfalls such as: your business could lose interest that you could have earned, even if you put it into a low interest savings account. You can't take advantage of purchase discounts from your vendors if the funds are not immediately available or they are paying on terms. You may lack the capital to produce the next job, and may be forced to decline profitable deals from good payers.

Some reasons for extending credit are to meet or beat the competition. If your competitors are extending credit you may want to offer the same. It may be more convenient for your customers to be billed for your product or service. Extending credit may also increase sales. You can also use extending credit as a way to establish new accounts.

Keep in mind that extending credit will take more time and money than you are already extending. Someone will have to take the time to check references, process credit applications, set up new accounts, and maybe collect on accounts that you do extend credit to that don't pay on time.

Get the following information from a business and/or consumer seeking credit:

- Business's and owner's name
- Length of time they have been in business
- Address, length of time at that address, and a former address
- Balance sheets and/or IRS returns
- Phone numbers of business and principal's or residence
- Bank name, address, phone numbers
- Credit references, personal and business
- Employer name, address, and phone numbers
- Length of time at current employment

- Marital status, name, and employment information on spouse
- Total monthly household income
- Social Security number and/or Federal ID#

This information can be in the form of a credit application or contract you may have drawn up. Be sure to have the business owner or consumer sign the document and date it. Keep the original and always give the consumer a copy.

You will then need to verify the information that has been supplied to you. You can run a report with Dun & Bradstreet if the applicant is a business (www.dnb.com/us). You can call all references listed, the applicant's bank, and place of employment. If you are a member of a credit bureau you can check with a credit bureau on the accuracy of the information supplied to you. If you find any information is not true, you should deny credit. Check out www.smallbusiness.dnb. com. D&B collects, aggregates, edits, and verifies data from thousands of sources daily.

Once you decide you will grant credit, you need to put your credit terms in writing. Always have your credit terms on your invoices and statements.

Once you have invoiced your customer you need to keep a close eye on your accounts receivables. You can print a penalty on your invoices such as charging a 12 percent penalty on invoices over 30 days past due. You can make phone calls or send reminder notices to any accounts that are past due. If your business does grant credit, you must comply with federal laws affecting credit sales to consumers. Also, states are beginning to adopt consumer credit laws that mirror federal law. One of the laws you should become familiar with is the Truth In Lending Act. This law requires you to disclose your exact credit terms to credit applicants and regulates how you advertise consumer credit. Among the items you must disclose to a consumer who buys on credit are monthly finance charges, your annual interest rate, your terms or when payment is due, the total price, and the price if any late fees are added.

Another law is the Fair Credit Billing Act. This law explains what to do if a customer claims you made a mistake in your billing. The customer must notify you within 60 days after you mailed the first bill containing the claimed error. You must respond within 30 days unless the dispute has already been resolved. You must also conduct a reasonable investigation and, within 90 days of getting the customer's letter, explain why your bill is correct or else correct the error.

The Equal Credit Opportunity Act, this law exists so that you will not discriminate against a credit applicant on the basis of race, color, religion, national origin, age, sex, or marital status. The Act does leave you free to consider legitimate factors in granting credit, such as the applicant's financial status (earnings and savings) and credit record. Despite the prohibition on age discrimination, you can deny a consumer who hasn't reached the legal age for entering into contracts.

The Fair Credit Reporting Act is intended to protect consumers from having their eligibility for credit marred by incomplete or misleading credit report information. The laws gives consumers the right to a copy of their credit reports. If they see an inaccurate item, they can ask that it be corrected or removed. If the business reporting the credit problem doesn't agree to a change or deletion or if the credit bureau refuses to make it, the consumer can add a 100-word statement to the file explaining his or her side of the story. This becomes a part of any future credit report.

The Fair Debt Collection Practices Act is geared mostly toward third party collectors. Small businesses are more directly affected by state laws that apply directly to collection methods used by a creditor.

More Credit and Collections Tips

FIVE EASY STEPS TO HELP YOU GET PAID!

THERE ARE ALWAYS SOME COMPANIES that have past due invoices and can't seem to get them paid. They might be quietly waiting to get paid not wanting to contact the client for fear of appearing "desperate." Sometimes a big part of the problem is no response. It is bad enough when you are not getting paid, but when orders keep coming in and you are not getting any acknowledgement to your collection efforts, you just can't keep processing orders.

There are steps you can take to get paid on those past due invoices and keep new invoices current.

Step #1 Gather together all the past due invoices, and stamp them PAST DUE.

Step #2 If you have an email address or phone number with a contact name for your client, email them or call them and give them the information on the past due invoices and let them know their account is on hold.

Step #3 Mail the invoices to your client with return receipt requested or send them in a flat rate Priority Mail envelope with delivery confirmation.

Step #4 Send a letter with these invoices stating the age, invoice numbers, their PO#, your account #, total amount due, and any other pertinent information.

Step #5 Tell them their account is on hold and you will not be shipping any more products or providing any services to them until these invoices are paid. You can include a self-addressed envelope and state that you have enclosed an envelope for them to send their check. Give them a date to have this paid to you.

Once they have received the package,

email or call them. Ask them what they are doing with the invoices. Ask them questions such as:

- Do they have to be approved by someone else?
- If they have to be approved, who has to approve them and when will they give them to that person? Get that person's direct number if possible. Find out if that person signs the checks.
- Are there any discrepancies with the invoices?
- When will the check be cut? When can you call back for the check number?

Once all the past due balances are cleared up, you need to think about future invoices. Do you want to extend credit again or do you want to have pre-payment or payment at the time of the order? Whatever you decide put it in writing. If you can both sign the agreement, that is even better. Remember, having a credit policy in place tells people you mean business.

HOW TO AVOID GETTING STIFFED; IMPROVING YOUR COLLECTION PROCEDURES

Some businesses have slow-paying customers or past due balances because they didn't "train" their customers in the beginning.

It is important that your customers know your credit policy and/or terms of payment, *before* they become a customer. Reiteration of your credit policy, when payment is overdue, is a good step to take in trying to obtain payment. Always ask for payment when it is justly due. Remember:

- You should never extend credit to a new customer without having them fill out a credit application and go through the credit approval policy. Once you extend credit, it is important to maintain accurate records on an accounts payment history.
- Adhere to your collection policies no matter what. You cannot see the future or changing market conditions. Try to keep current with trade reports pertaining to specific companies and industries.
- Change your collection letters frequently. You can make them stronger and more action oriented.
- Discourage payments on account or changes in payment terms. Too many payment plans or changed payment terms can impair your cash flow.
- When you receive payments "on account" be sure to follow up right way with a letter or phone call thanking them for their payment and telling them what their new balance is and when to send it.
- On large accounts call or send a reminder just a few days after terms if they get delinquent.
- Ask to speak to a manager or owner when making collection calls rather than speaking to a secretary or receptionist. Go right for the decision maker.
- If a customer disputes the quality of merchandise, service, price, or delivery, you should attempt to resolve this right way. Insist they pay the portion of the bill that they are not disputing while you work out the disputed problem.
- If all else has failed you may want to refer the account to an outside collection agency.

TIPS TO GET YOUR ENVELOPE OPENED

Having been a bill collector and having been a debtor, I know how many envelopes are thrown away unopened. You carefully word your letter, check it over and over, make changes until you think it is perfect. Then it never sees the light of day.

Your envelope has to be different in a way that gets it opened. The envelope is the first impression. It needs to scream "OPEN ME!" An invoice or a bill doesn't scream that. It is your job to make it scream and get a reaction. If you can't get your envelopes opened, you're wasting your time on what is inside. Try these things:

- Choose envelopes that are different shapes, colors, and sizes.
- Design the envelope for "eye flow." Studies show people will look at their name, any comments below the return address, and then the postage.
- Make sure the name and address are correct; check spelling!
- Stamp or print something on the outside of the envelope in a larger font and/or color.
- Use many stamps rather than a metered piece or one stamp.
- Stamp the envelope FIRST CLASS to show importance.

TEN STEPS FOR BUSINESS OWNERS TO TAKE IF YOU ARE THE VICTIM OF IDENTITY THEFT

Be aware that 40 million crooks obtained credit card numbers this past year, "Be Suspicious." Also be aware that most identify theft is not reported, especially when it involves family members, so the statistics are off. These statistics show that consumers lost $5 billion last year when in actuality it is closer to $50 billion. There have been an estimated 9.9 million victims in America.

In a recent article in *MSN Money* their research showed that 32 percent of people said they had been a victim of identity fraud by a friend or family, and 13 percent were victimized by a co-worker. Beware! These people know your patterns and habits.

- Contact the fraud departments of the three major credit bureaus, to place a fraud alert on your credit file.
- Close all accounts that have been affected and request copies of fraud-dispute forms and complete and return immediately. Keep copies!
- File a police report in each jurisdiction the theft occurred.
- Send copies of the report to your creditors or anyone that requires proof of the crime.
- File a complaint with the FTC (800-IDTHEFT or www.consumer.gov/idtheft) and Post Office.
- Contact the Identity Theft Resource center at 858-693-7935 or www.idtheftcenter.org.
- Request a new driver's license from the state of motor vehicles and have a fraud report attached to your driving record.
- Notify check-verification firms about any fraudulent checks:
  International check service 800-526-5380
  Telecheck 800-927-0755
  Certegy Check Services 800-437-5120
  Call 1-888-CALL-FCC and file a complaint.

- Change your passwords and PIN immediately.

RESOURCES TO PROTECT YOUR BUSINESS AND YOURSELF FROM IDENTITY THEFT

There is a new bill that is being passes. It is a very weak bill but if passed, it will prohibit using a Social Security number for identification purposes. This bill takes effect in 2006.

If you feel you have been a victim of identity fraud, contact the Department of Justice, Consumer Protection Division. They offer mediation with identity theft; they also have a hot line for consumers that is available 8-5 Monday – Friday. They maintain a database of written complaints that goes back to 1998. They offer seminars to schools, seniors, or your group.

U.S. Postal Inspection Service
www.usps.com/postalinspectors

Federal Trade Commission
www.consumer.gov.idtheft
877-IDTHEFT or TTY – 202-326-2502

U.S. Secret Service
www.secretservice.gov

Department of Justice
www.usdoj.gov/criminal/fraud/idtheft

Federal Deposit Insurance Corporation
www.fdic.gov/consumers

Equifax
www.exuifax.com
800-525-6285

Experian
www.experian.com

888-397-3742

Trans union
www.transunion.com
800-680-7289

Social Security Administration Fraud Hotline
PO Box 17768
Baltimore, MD 21235
800-269-0271
www.socialsecurity.gov

North American Securities Agency Administrators (NASAA)
www.nasaa.org

Better Business Bureau
www.search.bbb.org/search.html

United States Postal Service
www.usps.com

National Do Not Call Registry
www.donotcall.gov
888-382-1222

Direct Marketing Association Consumer Assistance
www.dmaconsumers.org/consumerassistance.html
Registering by mail is FREE and registering online is $5.00. To remove your name from national mailing lists by mail:

Mail Preference Service
Direct Marketing Association
PO Box 643
Carmel, NY 10512

Identity Theft Resource Center
www.idtheftcenter.org
858-693-7935

International check service
800-526-5380

Telecheck
800-927-0755

Certegy Check Services
800-437-5120

Internet Fraud Complaint Center
http://www.ifccfbi.gov/index.asp

Fight Identity Theft
www.fightidentitytheft.com/

HOW DID A THIEF GET MY NAME? DON'T BE A VICTIM OF IDENTITY THEFT!

How do these people get my name? If you have a credit card, your name is sold to third parties. If you do not want this to happen, you must contact your credit card companies to inform them that you do not want your information sold. Check the privacy notice that comes with your bill. If you enter contests, your information becomes public. Also, when you buy a new product, and fill out the warranty cards, those companies sell that information you provide to other companies. Since when does your toaster manufacturer need to know you household's annual income to extend a warranty on your toaster? Thieves use dumpster digging, phishing, and pharming to obtain your information. Things they steal from your trash include:

- Pre-approved credit card offers—they complete them and have the card sent to them at a different address.
- Loan applications—they complete the application and have the money sent to a phony address.
- Bank statements—they then have your

bank account number and can print counterfeit checks

Becky Palmer, a Consumer Credit Counselor, knew of someone who had their wallet stolen, and the thief used the credit card to buy a $5000.00 gift card at Wal-Mart, this then become very hard to trace.

People that are more at risk are senior citizens, people with disabilities, and immigrants, but remember that everyone, including children, are at risk. Senior citizens are home all day; they might get a phone call from a fake charity asking for money. Immigrants are desperate for credit; they may have just arrived in the US and know they need credit to do anything and are not aware of these scams. People with disabilities are at home, and may become a victim of phone or online fraud. There have also been cases of home care providers taking advantage of their clients. Remember, it is not always a stranger that can steal someone's identity. Did you know children can be victims of identity theft? This could affect or ruin their credit before they even are able to build up credit for themselves. There have been cases of parents using a child's name for their electric bill or phone bill when they have bad credit or owe the utility company money. Thieves will obtain the Social Security number of these children then use that number to get credit cards and rack up purchases.

Some of these scammers will call you and say they are from a fictitious charity. They will offer to have your contribution automatically deducted from your checking account and will ask for your routing number, bank name, and account number. DO NOT GIVE OUT THIS INFORMATION! If you pick up a call from a telemarketer, ask them the following questions and if they are a fraud, they will hang up quickly.

- Who do you work for? They will try to give you the name of the fake charity here, so ask them "who pays your salary?"
- How much of my donation (percentage) goes to this charity and what is the rest of the money used for?" If they are for real, they can easily give you this information.
- What is the charity's full name, address, and phone number?

Once you have the above information you can check with the state attorney general's office or secretary of state to see if the charity is registered. Also check the charity's rating thru the Better Business Bureau at www.give.org.

HOW YOU CAN PREVENT IDENTITY THEFT?

How can you prevent Identity theft from happening to you? Never leave your receipt or slip in the ATM or gas pump. Pay attention to your habits, lock up or organize and file your bills and bank statements. Shred them using a cross shredder before throwing them away.

Some steps you can take to avoid becoming a victim of Identity theft are:

- Get a copy of your credit report from all three credit bureaus. (FREE as of 9/1/05!)

Experian
PO Box 2002
Allen TX 75013 www.experian.com
888-397-3742

Equifax,
PO Box 740241

Atlanta, GA 30348 www.equifax.com
800-685-1111

Trans Union
PO Box 4000
Chester, PA 19016
www.transunion.com
866-887-2673

- Opt out of mailing lists by contacting the credit bureaus above.
- Opt out by reading the privacy notice that comes with your credit card and following the instructions.
- Call the national Do Not Call Registry at 1-888-382-1222 or visit www.donotcall.gov. Be sure to call from the number you want to register.
- Do not carry your Social Security card in your wallet.
- Do not print your Social Security number on your checks.
- Do not get your Social Security number printed on your drivers' license.
- Do not carry your Medicaid card with you, Medicaid #'s are your Social security number
- Delete any emails from Nigeria, or lottery or prize notifications before opening.
- Stop credit card offers: 888-5-OPT-OUT.
- Remove your name from national mailing lists by visiting www.the-dma.org or write to: Mail Preference Service
PO Box 643
Carmel, NY 10512
- Install firewall and virus protection software on your computer.
- Password protect your computer and private personal files

- Format your hard drive or physically destroy when disposing of your old computer.
- When you order new checks, get your first initial printed on them instead of your first name.
- Use a cross shredder to shred your bills and bank statements or any junk mail.
- Take your mail to the post office or secure mail box rather than leaving it in a rural box.
- Use only one designated credit card for online purchases.
- Be sure all online purchases are made through a secure server – notice the "lock" icon and how the URL address changes from http to https. The S means SECURE.
- Do not carry your PIN # in your wallet.
- Do not use your date of birth as a password or PIN.
- Do not give out personal or financial information over the phone.
- Grind up or shred back-up CD's you are throwing away.
- Check your online banking account at least 3 times a week and change your password often.

Index